WE STAND
FULLY IDENTIFIED IN THE
NEW CREATION
RENEWED IN KNOWLEDGE
ACCORDING TO THE
PATTERN
OF THE EXACT
IMAGE OF OUR
CREATOR
(COL *3:10*, MIR)

Beyond Human
Justin Paul Abraham
www.companyofburninghearts.com

Cover art by Oliver Pengilley
www.oliverpengilley.co.uk

Published by Seraph Creative in 2016
United States / United Kingdom / South Africa / Australia
www.seraphcreative.org

Typesetting & Layout by Feline
www.felinegraphics.com

Printed in USA, UK and RSA, 2016

ISBN 978-0-9944335-5-8

BEYOND HUMAN

JUSTIN PAUL ABRAHAM

 PUBLISHED BY SERAPH CREATIVE

DEDICATION

In honour of

ERIC JOHN DAVIES
1928 - 2011

who left a spiritual legacy
for generations to come

CONTENTS

PROLOGUE: THE DAWN

Have you noticed the world is rapidly changing?

Artificial intelligence is swiftly approaching human levels of awareness.

Science is stepping into quantum understanding of the transdimensional cosmos.

Genetics is being mapped and manipulated, forcing change to the nature of species.

Radical movements are sweeping earth bringing massive societal changes.

We are in the era of the greatest change for centuries - perhaps the greatest time of change in the history of mankind.

Humanity is awakening.

The long slumber is over. The hardness has melted.

The signs are everywhere that our species is destined for something greater.

USA prophet Larry Randolph writes:

The world is fast approaching an era of supernatural awareness. Fortune-telling, telepathic communication, palmistry, horoscope predictions, and other paranormal activities are experiencing a revival of popularity.

Our desire to hear from the other side has spawned a host of psychics for hire and other mediums of celebrity status that reportedly see our past, predict our future, and communicate with

our dead relatives. **On a daily basis we are bombarded with the sound of insight into the unknown.**

What does this tell us?[1]

I think it tells us capitalism, atheism and modernism have failed to hit the mark. The institutionalised control-system of religion hasn't met the spiritual need. We have more possessions than any previous generation, yet we have never felt emptier.

We are stirring as a species. The cry of the global prayer movements and houses of prayer over the last decades, is being answered. Heaven is responding.

There is an ache deep down inside that we are made for something more. A dream that simply doesn't go away. As the prophetic writer C.S. Lewis once said:

If I find in myself desires which nothing in this world can satisfy, the only logical explanation is that I was made for another world.[2]

That other world is calling. That other world is where we belong.

At first it was a gentle whisper echoing in the back of our minds, haunting our sub-conscious dreams. Now it is a shout. It booms loudly through high definition Hollywood super-movies, supernatural TV shows, mystical books and spirit-saturated culture.

The day of supernatural neutrality is over (Rick Joyner).[3]

The cloud is moving and we had best move with it (Patricia King).[4]

There is a Voice calling us as a species back to the Blueprint of our Design.

A Voice calling us out of ignorance into an expansive future beyond our wildest dreams. A future beyond the limitations of space and time, the mind and the physical body.

A future "Beyond Human".

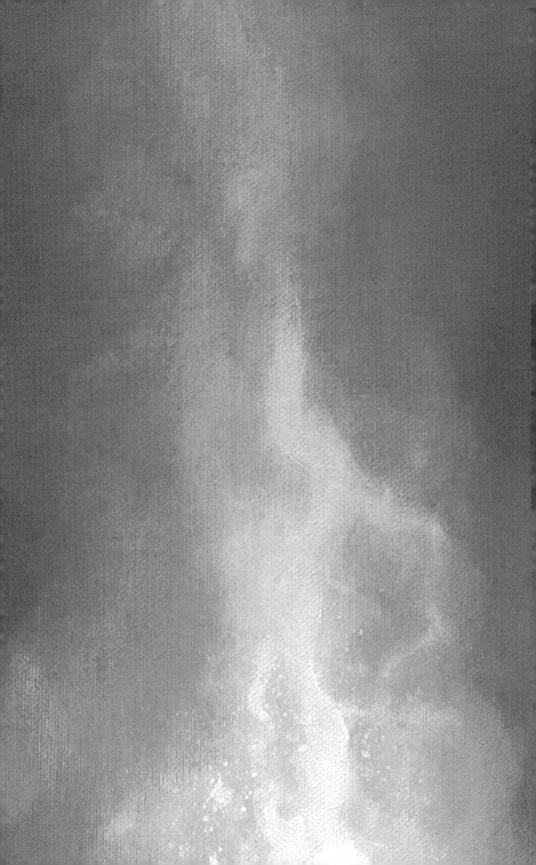

PART ONE:
INTRODUCTION

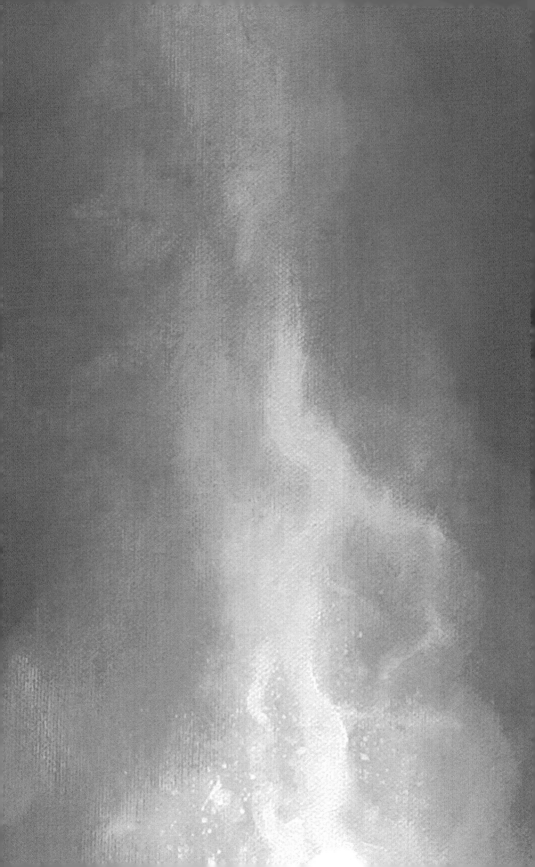

THE COMINGHARVEST

And it shall come to pass in the last days, God declares, that I will pour out of My Spirit upon ALL mankind (AMPC)... everyone (CJB)... all people (ERV) (Acts 2:17).

The storm clouds are gathering for the greatest outpouring of all time, a global invasion of great grace, producing earth-wide spiritual enlightenment and the healing of nations.

Many prophets over the last century have foreseen the coming extraordinary events, prophets like Paul Cain. Over many years, Paul saw repeated trance-like visions of the future. It was like watching a movie screen opening up in front of his face. In these profound spiritual experiences, Paul saw crowds filling stadiums caught up in ecstatic worship, the news media reporting day and night on the breathtaking signs, with major sports events cancelled to make room for the awakening. Unprecedented revival!

In September 1987, Rick Joyner (MorningStar Ministries) saw a sweeping panoramic vision of the future. In this unusual series of encounters, Rick saw an outpouring of the Spirit destined to eclipse every previous historic awakening. Rick writes about this in his book *Visions of the Harvest*:

In all nations, masses of people will be streaming to the Lord. The inflow will be so great in places that very young Christians will be pastoring large bodies of believers. Arenas and stadiums will overflow nightly as the believers come together to hear the apostles and teachers.

Great meetings that stir entire cities will happen spontaneously. Extraordinary miracles will be common while those considered great today will be performed almost without notice by young believers. Angelic appearances will be so common to the saints and a visible glory of the Lord will appear upon some for extended periods of time as power flows through them.

This harvest will be so great that no one will look back at the early church as a standard, but all will be saying that the Lord has saved his best wine for last! The early church was a first fruits offering; truly this is the harvest![1]

This promise of profound grace upon a generation is echoed in the words written by the prophet Isaiah. He gazed into the future with expectant joy.

God rises on you, his sunrise glory breaks over you. Nations will come to your light, kings to your sunburst brightness. Look up! Look around!... When you see them coming you'll smile - big smiles! Your heart will swell and, yes, burst! (Is 60:1-3, MSG).

This love-tsunami may begin small with a few rising. When it gathers momentum and pulls the force of grace, the wave will be unstoppable and the impact global.

But [the time is coming when] the earth shall be FILLED with the knowledge of the glory of the Lord as the waters cover the sea (Hab 2:14, AMP).

ALL the ends of the world shall remember and turn to the Lord, and ALL the families of the nations shall worship before You (Psalms 22:27 KJV).

I love that word 'ALL'. It's time to put the all back into the Gospel!

What is coming is beyond the salvation of souls. It is an entire reformation of the world society, technology, human genetics, economics, lifestyle and spirituality. Even nature and animals will be encompassed by this change.

The Earth itself will be physically altered.

**Leopards will lie down with young goats,
and wolves will rest with lambs.
Calves and lions will eat together
and be cared for by little children (Is 11:6, CEV).**

A planet-wide shift into a higher frequency, a higher dimension, touching everyone.

Despite everything, all the mistakes, all the delays... Love never fails!

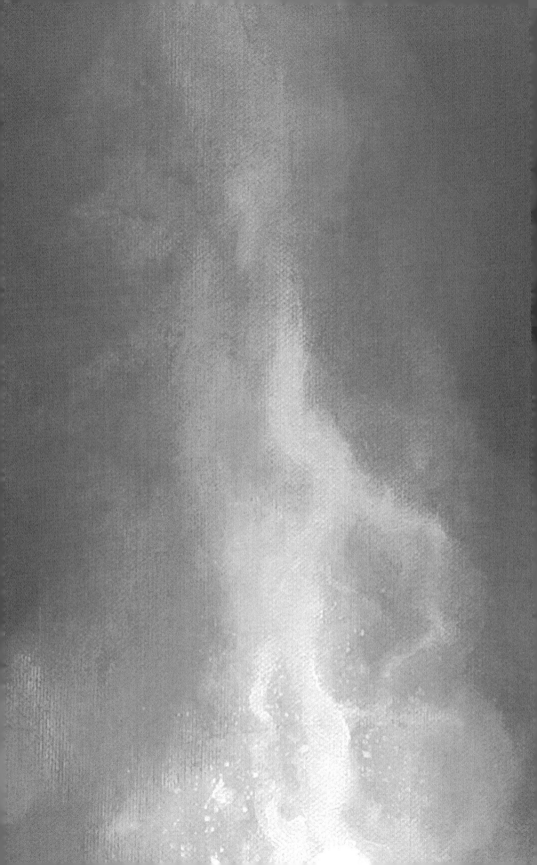

THE
KAINOS SONS

We see the original and intended pattern of our lives preserved in the Son. He is the firstborn from the same womb that reveals our genesis (Rom 8:29, MIR).

To shape the future, we must look again with child-like wonder at the Glorious Gospel! Contained in the inspirational letters of Paul are many mysteries. Hidden wisdom that must be understood today to help us advance. Small keys to big doors!

Searching for a word to describe the miraculous change Christ worked in the heart of humanity, Paul used the Greek word "KAINOS" being. A word I have grown to love.

Therefore, if any one is in UNION with Christ he is a NEW ("KAINOS") being (2 Cor 5:17, TCNT).

"KAINOS" is a very revealing word, a word that will help you grasp the enormous wonder of the Gospel. It will give you a grid for where we are going next as a planet and as a species.

Slow down and digest this. "KAINOS" doesn't just mean 'new' as in a replacement for the old. That's not the Gospel. Christ didn't come to just change Adam with another newer Adam of the same human nature. He wasn't like a smartphone upgrade. No way!

Jesus did not come here to create a newer replacement for the old fallen man. He came to destroy and end the old man and begin a brand new species of "KAINOS" design. A species "Beyond Human", living in Divine union with a limitless capacity to grow.

According to Strong's Biblical Dictionary[1] "KAINOS" means:

a new kind
unprecedented
novel
uncommon
unheard of

Did you see that? Unprecedented. I love that. It means:

"without previous instance; never before known or experienced; unexampled or unparalleled" (dictionary.com).

It's almost too much to handle. This is the joy of the Gospel! The world has never seen anything like us. Not even Adam before the fall can compare to what we are becoming. Yes, this is a mystery! Yes, there is so much more to know! We must be brave and explore!

Let's look at another definition to expand our understanding. We need to ask Holy Spirit to open the wonder! Vines Biblical Dictionary defines "KAINOS" as:

New as to form or quality, of different nature from what is contrasted as old.[2]

I know these are just words on a page. Stop, pause, try to mediate on what this means. There is such bliss hidden here. Deep mystical truths waiting to be discovered.

The implications are huge, well beyond the typical Sunday salvation message with 'a ticket to Heaven'. "KAINOS" is immortal and ever living, a metamorphosis.

You have been regenerated (born again), not from a mortal origin (seed, sperm), but from one that is immortal by the ever living and lasting Word of God (1 Pet 1:23, AMPC).

"KAINOS" is seeded by the DNA of God. It is an entirely NEW

CREATION, superseding and eclipsing what existed before. It is an order beyond the limitations of Earth life.

In this new creation life, your nationality makes no difference, or your ethnicity, education, or economic status - they matter nothing. For it is Christ that means everything as he lives in every one of us! (Col 3:11, PAS).

Free from Earth definitions - nationality - gender - genetics - these cannot define us any longer. We can't afford to see ourselves through that old lens anymore. As Paul said in 2 Corinthians 5:16:

Henceforward, we do not think of anyone in a merely human fashion (KNO).

We know no one simply as a man (WNT).

We don't evaluate people by what they have or how they look... Now we look inside, and what we see is that anyone united with the Messiah gets a fresh start, is created new (MSG).

We may work in the same office. Drink at the same Starbucks. Watch the same movies. Enjoy the same curry! But we are not the same anymore. We have to stop pretending to be something we are not. We are immersed in the burning layers of the Divine.

The exact life in Christ is now repeated in us. We are being co-revealed in the same bliss; we are joined in oneness with him, just as his life reveals you, your life reveals Him (Col 3:4, MIR)!

Did you see that? Oneness... I love it!!

We are in a co-world with Christ, filled with ever-living saints, numerous angels and indescribable wonders. A reality of time-bending possibilities and many dimensional planes of existence. Infused with supernatural powers, wisdom, knowledge and much more. An expansive world beyond our wildest dreams.

If anyone is in Christ... he is in a NEW WORLD (BE).

How do we begin to walk in this? It's simple. Easy enough for a child to grasp. By faith we step into it. We believe Jesus is the Door that gives us FREE access (John 10:9). Given as a pure grace gift. We can do nothing to achieve it. He makes us righteous.

Out of sheer generosity he put us in right standing with himself. A pure gift. He got us out of the mess we're in and restored us to where he always wanted us to be. And he did it by means of Jesus Christ (Rom 3:21-26, MSG).

God made me alive together with Christ. How can any human effort improve on this? The terms co-crucified and co-alive defines me now. Christ in me and I in him! (Gal 2:19-20, MIR).

Humanity has been co-crucified with Christ. It is finished and done. We are co-alive.

The mysterious "Beyond Human" race has arrived.

MYSTICAL CO-MISSION

I will work miracles in the sky above and wonders on the Earth below (Acts 2:19, CEV).

Is the Gospel awakening your heart? I hope so. I hope you are getting expanded into the glorious life he prepared for you (John 10:10). A life of endless joy and redeemed innocence.

Jesus is God's grace embrace of the entire human race. So here we are, standing tall in the joyful bliss of our redeemed innocence! We are God's dream come true! (Rom 5:2, MIR).

I want to take the progressive logic of the last chapters even further. I am fully persuaded by the Gospel. I have seen glimpses of the future and it is glorious.

How quickly it is coming! We are closer than we imagined!

And do this, knowing the time, that now it is high time to awake out of sleep; for now our salvation is nearer than when we first believed. The night is far spent, the day is at hand (Rom 13:11-12).

Are you ready? Ready for the spiritual revolution? Patricia King writes:

Perhaps some of what the Lord is about to do will shock and awe many people. As in past historical moves of revolution, there will be those who resist and harden their heart, desiring to hold on to old ways and mind-sets. Change is often difficult because it forces us to rethink hardened opinions and be willing to remove ourselves

from the rut of comfortable lifestyles. However, in spite of those who resist the revolution, there will be those who embrace it, jumping on board and following Jesus into new and uncharted territory. Some things that God will manifest in these coming days have never been done before, things that will stretch our imagination and challenge our intellect.[1]

We better get ready to be stretched! Like the time of the Gospel stories again, I think we're all going to get brain-fried!! Just look at what the people of Jesus' day said:

We have seen wonderful
and strange
and incredible
and unthinkable
things today! (Luke 5:26, AMPC)

This is where we are going again. I keep hearing "crazy days" in the Spirit.

"Do what I did and more!" Jesus still cries. Heaven wants us to succeed.

I assure you that the man who believes in me will do the same things that I have done, yes, and he will do even greater things than these, for I am going away to the Father. Whatever you ask the Father in my name, I will do - that the Son may bring glory to the Father. And if you ask me anything in my name, I will grant it. (John 14:12, PHI).

Just think about it - doing what Jesus did and more.

We've become experts at teaching in the Church. We have the prophetic ministry, healing rooms, counselling and deliverance. We prophesy, care for the poor, engage in social action and preach salvation.

But why did the Church stop there? Did someone draw an invisible line?

For nearly two thousands years most of the Church has held back on the shores of unbelief. Listening to hours of preaching, yet aiming for less than the Design.

Change is here. The present expression of Christianity is being transformed over the next decades. Whatever comes next will never be spiritually irrelevant again.

Are you ready for it? Rick Joyner says:

As we proceed toward the conclusion of this age, the conflict between light and darkness will become increasingly supernatural. The day when it was possible to take a neutral stance toward the supernatural is over.[2]

In the next chapters we are going to explore some of the amazing "KAINOS" works the modern Church has neglected. Open your capacity to dream. Engage your heart to experience. Awaken your desire for maximum fulfilment in your lifetime.

Step by step we will examine different elements of new creation realities. We will cover topics like shifting dimensions, living beyond food and sleep, infused knowledge, seeing remote events, walking with angels, miraculous transports and more.

We won't cover every possibility in this one volume. That would be one BIG book. I've kept it short. Maybe I will add more to the list with future editions.

I've aimed to teach each chapter based on three pillars - Jesus as the ultimate Blueprint, the saints as examples we can follow, and then modern stories from people with integrity. I'm hoping this will give you confidence in the authenticity of what I've written.

Each chapter can be read alone as a meditation or you can go through them in series. You can jump in and jump out of the book however you please.

You may end this book with more questions than answers - but that's okay. All true revelation should provoke an awareness that there's more to discover. Just embrace the beauty of mystery. That's the best way.

It's not a perfect book. I'm sure there are refinements to be made in future editions. However, it is written with passion and heart. It is written from my intimacy with Jesus.

I hope you enjoy it.

PART TWO:
BEYOND HUMAN

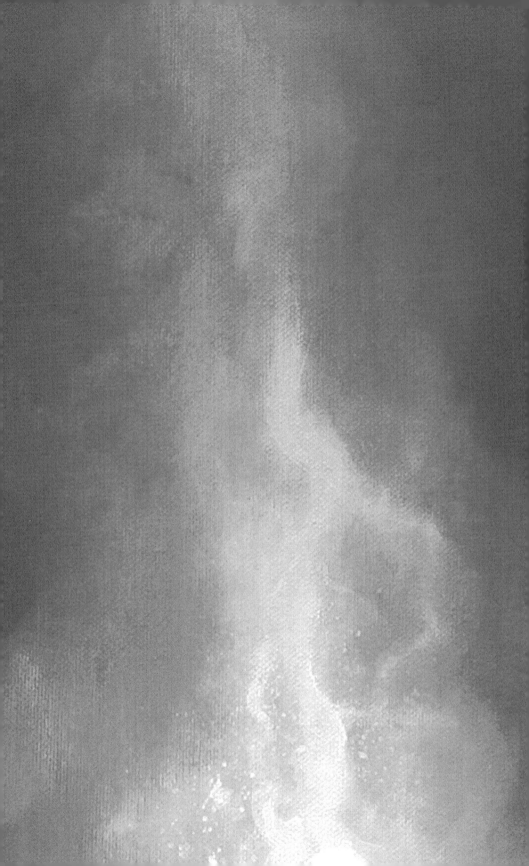

LIVING FROM ZION

"We must forge the future from the unseen." - Paul Keith Davis[1]

Did you ever watch the Matrix movie? If you haven't seen it yet, try it out, you'll like it! I really recommend it. I truly believe it is a prophetic vision for the Ecclesia.

It's themes are saturated with revelation - from overcoming the system, altering the physical world and jumping over buildings to downloading instant knowledge, stopping bullets, and flying through the sky!

But the key idea in the film - something I want us to explore now - is the idea that the visible world is just one layer of reality. That behind this seen layer is the hidden "real world" that governs and shapes that world. What we would call the Heavenly Realms.

As we start Part 2, I want to examine the mysterious truth that we now live entangled into Heaven. A part of us is always there with Christ. In Him we have free access to the unseen. We can unplug from the Earth and spend time in Zion through the Spirit.

It's shocking! It's hard to understand. But we have to make this transition for what is coming. In some mysterious way we are already home, entwined with Christ:

If then you were raised with Christ, seek those things which are above, where Christ is, sitting at the right hand of God. Set your mind on things above, not on things on the earth. For you died,

and your life is hidden with Christ in God (Col 3:1-2).

To understand what has happened, let's look again at Christ, the Prototype of us.

We all agree Jesus came from Heaven. Right? This is where it gets interesting. Strangely, in some mystical way, Jesus did not completely leave Heaven. Some of His essence also remained. Don't panic, this is in the Bible! In John 3:12, Jesus tells Nicodemus this awe-inspiring secret:

If I have told you earthly things and you do not believe, how will you believe if I tell you heavenly things? No one has ascended to heaven but He who came down from heaven, *that is*, the Son of Man who is in heaven (John 3:12).

That must have cooked Nicodemus' noodle! Not only had Jesus talked about being born again. Weird enough! Jesus then added that he came from Heaven. Then blew the grid by saying he was still in Heaven whilst being with Nicodemus. I bet his head hurt!

Let's read it again in the AMPLIFIED:

And yet no one has ever gone up to heaven, but there is One Who has come down from heaven - the Son of Man [Himself], *Who is (dwells, has His home) in heaven.*

Incredible right?! Jesus was saying he was dwelling IN HEAVEN. It was his home. He revealed to Nicodemus a higher way of living. Jesus reinforced this idea when he said:

I speak what I have seen with My Father (John 8:38).

Where did Jesus see the Father? In Heaven of course - "Our Father in Heaven" (Luke 11:2). This is how Jesus learned. He would turn into the unseen to see and be taught.

Whole nights were dedicated to being in the Spirit with the Father.

For the "KAINOS" race, Heaven is ground-zero where we get taught, refreshed, illuminated and transformed.

For Jesus it was NATURAL to shift dimensions to engage the heavenly world. He had free access there as a mature Son. Here's just one example in John 17:1.

He lifted up His eyes to heaven and said, Father, the hour has come.

Dig deeper and you will find the phrase "lifted up his eyes" literally means:

Jesus was "raised on high (*epairo*)" to where "God dwells (*ouranos*)"

He shifted up dimensions to pray. He was in Heaven and on Earth. This is what the Apostle John calls being 'in the Spirit' (Rev 1:10) and my friend Ian Clayton calls 'stepping through the veil'. It is normal for us as "KAINOS" sons to enter Heaven:

Let us therefore come boldly to the throne of grace, that we may obtain mercy and find grace to help in time of need (Heb 4:16).

Death doesn't open this reality up for us. No! It is Jesus who gives us free access now:

I am the door. If anyone enters by Me, he will be saved, and will go IN and OUT and find pasture (John 10:9).

We can step in and step back out! This is "KAINOS" dimensional shifting.

In the past visiting Heaven was considered rare, just for prophets. This too is going to change. In fact going up will become so widespread that Ecclesia all over the world will be ascending together and seeing one another. It's true! The Bible says it plainly:

MANY people shall come and say, "Come, and let us go up to the mountain of the Lord, to the house of the God of Jacob; He will teach us His ways, and we shall walk in His paths." For out of Zion shall go forth the law, and the word of the Lord from Jerusalem

(Is 2:3).

Many will go into the heavenly Zion as citizens of the household of God.

Now, therefore, you are no longer strangers and foreigners, but fellow citizens with the saints and members of the household of God (Eph 2:19).

This is the Order of Melchizedek. A heavenly people moving from the unseen. The sharp oracle word of the Lord coming from Zion to shape the Earth. This is where we are now poised, the horizon of a new world. This is the Pattern of Christ.

And He said to him, "Most assuredly, I say to you, hereafter you shall see heaven open, and the angels of God ascending and descending upon the Son of Man." (John 1:51).

Jesus is the Open Heavens. In mystic union we also have free access to the Open Heavens. Like John on the isle of Patmos, we can be in the Spirit and turn to hear a Voice, to see the seven Lamps and ascend even higher again through the open Door.

And having turned I saw seven golden lampstands, and in the midst of the seven lampstands *One* like the Son of Man, clothed with a garment down to the feet and girded about the chest with a golden band (Rev 1:12-13).

Everywhere we travel to speak, there are a growing number of people having similar heavenly encounters. Many people are seeing into the unseen world of saints and angels. They are visiting and participating in the Courts, the Libraries, the Councils of God, the War Rooms, walking in Eden and more. It really is a marker of great change.

I have seen in visions and dreams that mystic hubs will emerge all over the Earth, connected together in God. We will see more than any other generation before us that there really is only one unified family in Heaven and on Earth (Eph 3:15). We are One.
This convergence will be powerful beyond anything we have seen

before. It will shock the world back into zeal for God with energy, life and joy!

Pastor Roland Buck tasted this dimension decades ago. Roland was studying and praying in his church office, preparing for the Sunday morning service. Suddenly at 10:30pm he was hijacked to Heaven![2]

I had my head down on my arm at the desk, when suddenly, without warning, I was taken right out of that room! I heard a voice say: "Come with me into the Throne Room where the secrets of the universe are kept!" I didn't have time to answer; space means nothing to God! It was like a snap of the fingers - boom - and I was right there!

Roland found Heaven was far more relaxed, light and happy than he ever imagined. God talked with him face-to-face and invited him to ask questions. It was beautiful.

During this visit, God truly gave me a glorious glimpse of the hidden secrets of the universe; of matter, energy, nature and space...

Roland felt he was there for several months or even longer. Amazingly when he returned to his church office only five Earth minutes had actually passed!

Suddenly I came back into my office, and saw myself with my head on my desk where I had been praying. Until that very instant, I thought I was in the Throne Room in my body, but I was not! The Lord has a wonderful sense of humour, and there is a lot of laughter and joy in heaven. I could see the back of my head, and I remarked, "Lord, I certainly did not know the back of my head was getting that white!"

I love that story. In the time it took to make a coffee, Roland Buck was in heaven for months and infused with knowledge of future events, insights into mysteries, and had over 2,000 scriptures burned into his memory. That's the kind of coffee break I'd like to have!
God gave me special illumination in over 2,000 verses of the Bible.

Instantly I knew these verses and their scriptural references by memory. I have no way to explain how it was done! I don't need to recall them - it's like seeing them any time I desire.

I'm telling you, sudden change is coming to us. People all over the globe are going to have similar experiences to Roland Buck. It will shatter the status quo and break the shackles of religion.

There is a "KAINOS" race emerging who will be sustained by the atmosphere of Heaven. Not only will they live in the Spirit, but ultimately part of them will remain in Heaven always.

Rick Joyner says:

There is a door standing open in Heaven, and there is an invitation for us to go through it. Those who answer this call will be caught up into the Spirit, with the result that they will always be seeing the One who sits on the throne. This is the ultimate purpose of all true prophetic revelation - seeing the glorious, risen Christ and the authority that he now has over all.[3]

Someone I believe who is touching this is Nancy Coen, a powerful missionary to the Islamic world. I once asked her how often she went to Heaven. She smiled and said:

Honey, the truth is I'm always in Heaven.

Her eyes shone and I knew it was true. She shines with the glory. Nancy has literally spent hundreds of hours being taught by Jesus, saints and angels in Heaven.

The late Bob Jones is another modern mystic that blurred the boundaries between Heaven and Earth. Bob used to joke about people waiting to be raptured at the second coming, when he would be raptured to Heaven five times a day! For Bob this was normal. He was God's friend, and friends get to see each other often!

Father, I want those you gave me to be with me, right where I am,

so they can see my glory, the splendour you gave me, having loved me long before there ever was a world (John 17:24, MES).

Jesus' longing is begging to be answered! Not when we die, but whilst we are alive!

Although there is so much more I could say, space is short. I want to end this chapter with one more story from the saints. You may know this group already? They were called the "Golden Candlestick". Prophet James Maloney was an eye-witness to what happened during their heavenly prayer times:

As soon as everyone began singing in tongues, the power of God fell like a heavy, thick fog. It was overwhelming. I could hear the people, but I couldn't see them. It took a few minutes for my eyes to adjust enough to see the person next to me...

The ceiling was concealed in a purple, swirling cloud - sometimes feathers were whirling inside the cloud. Out of the cloud, one could often hear the audible laughter of exultant children. It truly was an open heavens, a spiritual portal like Jacob's Ladder. There were numerous times the four-and-twenty elders were a part of the worship.

And just a consistent coming and going of angelic hosts... There were firelights (the only word I can use to describe them) which were the angels dropping down from the cloud above to the floor below. When the firelights struck the ground, one could see the angels' feet appear out of the flames.[4]

This group blurred dimensions for over fifty years, travelling physically into Heaven, returning with sandals and clothes entwined with jewels and golden thread. They demonstrated what is coming globally to the Earth.

Seem too good to be true? This is the Gospel!

Rick Joyner says:

This is not fantasy. True Christianity is the greatest adventure that anyone can ever have on this Earth. True church life, the way it was intended to be is a supernatural experience. It is life from another realm beyond this earth that brings true life to the Earth.[5]

The invitation has been given for us to follow the footsteps of Enoch, Elijah, John and the saints. How do we begin? I have learned that it is simple - through FAITH we enter in. Simply believe! By faith Enoch was taken!

Because of faith Enoch was caught up *and* transferred to heaven (Heb 11:5, AMPC).

Faith is believing that God has hidden us in Heaven in Christ (Col 3:3). That God wants us to go there experientially. The Door is always open. We are invited to join in with Zion. We are clean, holy and accepted in the Beloved. From this posture of innocence we step in through the veil.

Faith is taking the first step even when you don't see the whole staircase.[6]

My friend Ian Clayton teaches a very simple way to activate stepping through the veil. Ian says, take a physical step forward into the realm of Heaven[7], move your body and believe you are actually stepping in and back out of Zion. Imagine each time you do this you are crossing dimensions. Engage with Heaven by faith.

Through practise your spiritual senses will be activated. You will begin to have new experiences. This is the law of honour and focus. It is how Enoch started his journey into Heaven, through simple child-like faith. Eventually God took Enoch there permanently. Enoch is now ever-living in an expanded glorious state. Don't you want that?!

Have a go today.
Just take that small step.
You belong in Zion!

ANGELIC COMMUNITY

You have come to thousands of angels gathered together with joy (Heb 12:22, EXB).

In the last Chapter we talked about 'Living from Zion'. I hope you enjoyed it!

I love writing about Heaven and thinking about it. We have such a sweet Gospel! A Gospel that says we are included and innocent. We are accepted and loved. We are Home!

But now, wow! Everything has changed; you have discovered yourselves to be located in Christ. What once seemed so distant is now so near; his blood reveals your redeemed innocence and authentic genesis (Eph 2:13, MIR).

The joyful boasting in the finished works of Christ continues in this next chapter.

I'm going to talk about holy angels - our extended community in the new creation. A mysterious beautiful family that surrounds us and is actively involved in everything we do.

This is our "KAINOS" hidden community. A holy community that loves us very much and has our best interests at heart. A family that is cheering us on with endless encouragement.

Sounds good doesn't it?!

Then let's begin with the Gospel, the "Happy Message" once again.

As I've said before, repeating the words of Paul, the Gospel takes us out of the human condition and places us into a brand new eternal world, a "Beyond Human" reality.

If anyone is in Christ... he is in a new world (BE).

Religion conveys delay and distance, but Paul says the Gospel is NOW! The new has already begun. We are clean, changed and fit for the future today. Death does not qualify us. Jesus has already accomplished all that is needed at the Cross. He ripped the veil clean open. We now have free access to the unseen Kingdom worlds. This is the Gospel!

Now is the day of salvation! Heaven is as close as your hand.

For indeed, the kingdom of God is within you (Luke 17:21).

We should not be surprised by this! Heaven is at home in us.

All we have to do is open our hearts to his presence and the unseen dimensions around us will open up also. We become conscious of higher realms and other heavenly beings. In Christ we become aware of the angels!

We realise little by little, that these heavenly beings are intimately connected and caring towards us. In fact, we find they are everywhere we just didn't see it before.

He will give His angels [especial] charge over you to accompany and defend and preserve you in all your ways [of obedience and service] (Psalms 91:11, AMPC).

They watch over each one of us, and actually care about our lives and how well we are doing. They follow us around and defend us from evil. They secretly help us and help steer our steps. Isn't that amazing! I love it! We are surrounded!

This is where it gets exciting. In the past generation we were mostly unaware of angels, even when they were right in front of us. The Bible says people even had dinner with angels and didn't know it:

Some believers have shown hospitality to angels without being aware of it (Heb 13:2).

Good news! Ignorance is vanishing. We are awakening and becoming activated in cardio-gnosis (heart knowledge). We will not recognise angels through human perception any longer. The thin illusionary layer between us and them is vanishing as we mature as sons.

According to prophet Bobby Connor, the unseen spiritual membrane is thinning:

While ministering recently, I saw what appeared to be a very thin membrane in front of me. I asked, "Lord, what is this?" and the Lord replied, "It is the veil between the earthly realm and the spirit realm - and it is thinner than ever!"[1]

The saints of old knew how to see angels. But great grace is coming upon us to again live as they lived. Not because we deserve it, but because of God's plan and love for the Earth. Because it's high time to wake from slumber (Rom 13:11).

That might sound odd to some modern Christians, since we have been fed a lot of negativity and fear about engaging the angels. However, I want you to remember our aim is to be Biblical and follow Jesus. Again, as we go deeper, let's look at the Blueprint.

And He (Jesus) stayed in the wilderness (desert) forty days, being tempted [all the while] by Satan; and He was with the wild beasts, and the angels ministered to Him [continually] (Mark 1:13, AMPC).

This verse says that angels helped Jesus continually. Christ went lower, even as God, and received them. He welcomed their help. If the Eternal One honours and values angels, then we should follow his example. We should expect angelic ministry in our lives.

Again, this is very stretching, but Jesus is even more radical about this. In the next verse, Jesus describes his life as an access point for angels to engage the Earth realm. Listen carefully to these mystical words spoken by Jesus to Nathaniel:

Then he said to him, "Yes indeed! I tell you that you will see heaven opened and the angels of God going up and coming down on the Son of Man!" (John 1:51, CJB).

This is a box breaking radical verse! Jesus, the true Image of us, was an angelic hub! He was buzzing with angelic activity just like Jacob's ladder in Genesis 28:12. Crazy!

Can you imagine unseen angels swarming around him while he was healing the sick? While he was working miracles and calming the storm. I would love to have seen that!

We need to think differently about angels. For too long we have ignored them. Yet they are intrinsically connected to our story. They are part of our community.

How important are they? Just consider another moving story from the life of Jesus. In the Garden of Gethsemane, at possibly the darkest time in his life on Earth a special being came to help him:

He pulled away from them about a stone's throw, knelt down, and prayed, "Father, remove this cup from me. But please, not what I want. What do you want?" At once an angel from heaven was at his side, strengthening him. He prayed on all the harder. Sweat, wrung from him like drops of blood, poured off his face (Luke 22:41-44, MSG).

When the disciples weren't there for Jesus, the angels were. When his friends were sleeping, the angel was awake and ready to help. This story really touches me.

Have you ever felt alone? I think we all have.

Sometimes when I have been hurting and isolated, angels have come to our home. They have surrounded me, even touching my body filling me with energy.

Three times I have been awoken by an angel blowing on my face! I've heard them laughing, singing and even talking. I have seen them sparkle in the room, move like balls of light, stand like pillars of cloud. They truly are wonderful!

This is not new teaching. The saints of old were very familiar with the angels. Many of them knew their guardian angels by name. Some like Joseph of Cupertino would open the door for his and wait for him to pass through. Padre Pio would spend hours talking with his. Gemma Galgani would have angelic help getting into bed when she was weak.

Others like Columba would have face-to-face strategic councils with hosts of angels to discuss issues of government pertaining to Ireland and Britain. One of Columba's monks recorded this event:

Strange to tell - look! - there was suddenly a marvellous apparition, which the man could see with his own bodily eyes from his position on that nearby hill...

For holy angels, the citizens of the heavenly kingdom, were flying down with amazing speed, dressed in white robes, and began to gather around the holy man as he prayed.

After they had conversed a little with St. Columba, the heavenly crowd - as though they could feel they were being spied upon - quickly returned to the heights of heaven.[2]

The history books are bursting with other similar stories. How did we forget our past so easily? How did religion creep in and take away the power of the Gospel?

It's time for Christianity to remember angels are essential. We need them probably more than any previous generation ever has. We are in a global crisis. We need Heaven's helpers!

Randy Clark is one modern day missionary who understands the value of angels. Recently Randy came to our home city of Cardiff to speak. I heard him talk first hand about the importance of angels in miracles and harvest. What he said was illuminating!

I would suggest to you that on the day of Pentecost we got more than the baptism of the Spirit. We got more than a new relationship with Holy Spirit. We also entered into a new dispensation, a new covenant with the outpouring of the angels of God. I believe it is literally a new relationship that was opened up by the cross with the angels of God and the people of God and the Holy Spirit and the people of God.[3]

I would agree with Randy. The book of Acts shows a dynamic interchange with angels in the early church. One of my favourite stories is Peter escaping from prison.

Peter was sleeping between two soldiers. He was tied with two chains. Soldiers stood by the door and watched the prison. All at once an angel of the Lord was seen standing beside him. A light shone in the building. The angel hit Peter on the side and said, "Get up!" Then the chains fell off his hands. The angel said, "Put on your belt and shoes!" He did. The angel said to Peter, "Put on your coat and follow me."

Peter followed him out. He was not sure what was happening as the angel helped him. He thought it was a dream. They passed one soldier, then another one. They came to the big iron door that leads to the city and it opened by itself and they went through. As soon as they had gone up one street, the angel left him.

What happened next is pretty weird and often overlooked. Peter made it back to the church safe house. He knocked at the gate:

(The servant) ran in and announced that Peter stood before the gate. But they said to her, "You are beside yourself!" Yet she kept insisting that it was so. So they said, "It is HIS angel." Now Peter

continued knocking; and when they opened the door and saw him, they were <u>astonished</u>. (Acts 12:12-16).

I love that! They were more astonished it was Peter than his angel!

According to John Paul Jackson, this indicates angels were frequently present:

Now in early days this must have been a fairly common occurrence. We can surmise this, because when Peter was released from Prison and the servant girl went to open up the door... it was more likely an angel would appear than Peter would be out of prison.

You know it's common because there is something that did not happen. What was that? You are sitting at an evening meal. You're eating. Someone opens the door and says it's Peter's angel.

What are you going to do? Are you going to keep on eating? I'm not! I'm going to get up and go take a look at the angel. They didn't do that. They just kept eating. That tells you angelic appearances must have been fairly common.

Today they're not all that common yet. But I have this feeling they are going to get a lot more common.[4]

Isn't that amazing?! That should challenge us today. When did we last think like that?! When was it last normal for angelic beings to visit our gatherings in a visible form?

This is going to change! The Spirit has been progressively de-mystifying the angelic in our generation, preparing our hearts for a higher degree of engagement. We stand at the surge point, a moment of profound change, crossing the event horizon into destiny.

There are markers in the past for what's coming. One such testimony is what happened to American Pastor Roland Buck in the 1960s. He had regular face-to-face conversations with Gabriel and other angels.

Here's one of his first encounters:

Just after I had gone to bed, I noticed a bluish glow coming from the staircase. I knew it was too dim to be the light for the staircase, so I thought that possibly I had left a light on in one of the downstairs rooms. I got up, and started down to turn the light off. I was halfway down the stairs when the light flipped on!

Standing before me were two of the largest men I had ever seen in my life! I was shocked! I wasn't exactly frightened, but there was such a radiation of divine power which comes from them dwelling in the brightness of God's presence, that I could not stand up! My knees buckled and I started to fall! One of these huge beings reached out, took hold of me, and my strength returned!

He very simply told me he was the angel Gabriel! I was stunned! Could this be the same Gabriel I had read about in the Bible? The impact of the first visits were far less awesome than now, because here he stood, as clearly visible as any earthly man, and introduced himself as the angel Gabriel! It is impossible to describe my feelings of awe and wonder! Then he introduced me to the second angel whose name was Chroni! Chroni? That's a peculiar name. I never heard of that! ... I had never thought of all the angels having names, and as it turned out, all having different appearances! I asked Gabriel, "Why are the two of you here?" He merely said that the Holy Spirit had sent them, and then Gabriel immediately began telling me some beautiful truths.[5]

Roland Buck spent hours talking with Gabriel. They were far more relaxed and happy than you would have imagined. They even played with the dog!

We have so much to learn about angels. Don't you want to know more? We could learn so much from them.

I have seen in prophetic visions that in our lifetime we are going to talk face to face with angels just like Roland Buck. There will even be gatherings of Ecclesia where we will all see them. This will in fact be the new model for the apostolic roundtables. We will be in Heaven on Earth. Standing in the Council of God. Even seeing Jesus and the saints. Just like Enoch. It sounds far out, but it is not! It is simply a generation returning to the original design, walking with God face to face.

There's so much more I could say about the precious angels. Perhaps one day I will write a book about them. Share some crazy stories. That would be fun!

Maybe you're reading this now, you're hungry and you don't know where to start. I'm just beginning too. You're not alone. I'll tell you how it works for me. Maybe it will help you.

I started by saying to God, "I value angels. I want to walk with angels. Let them come Lord!" I then honoured the people who had already done this. People like Gary Oates who wrote the inspirational book *Open My Eyes Lord.*[6] I would say to God, "I honour Gary Oates. I want what he had. I want it!" I kept a posture of love, value and honour. This kind of approach attracts Heaven. You are powerful. God has given you choice. I chose to walk with angels, then asked for the permission from Heaven to experience them. I will never forget the first day they came as a group. But that's another story!

In the next chapter, we are going to expand on this transdimensional "KAINOS" community by talking about another exciting group of new friends you have in Christ - the 'Cloud of Witnesses' (the saints in Heaven).

You are not alone!

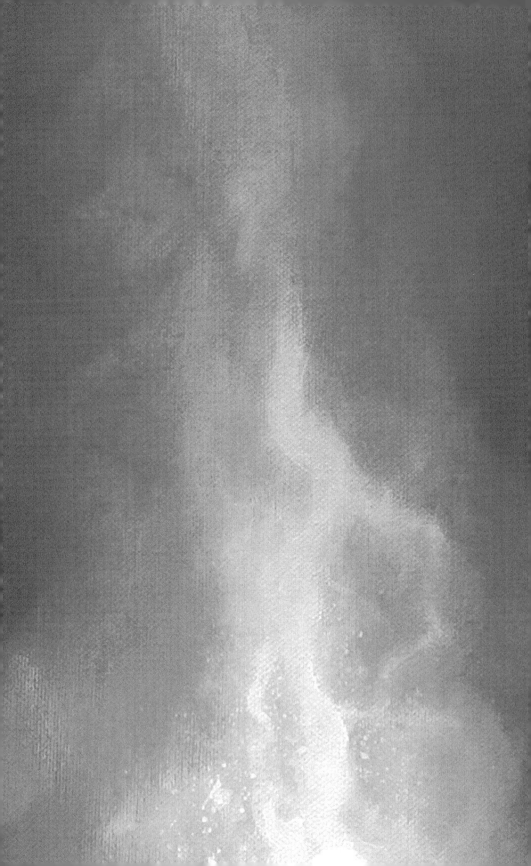

CLOUD OF WITNESSES

All these many people who have had faith in God are around us like a cloud (Heb 12:1, NLV).

Every journey begins with a small step. Don't be in a rush. It's important to enjoy the ride. Enjoy the process of growing into sonship. It really is beautiful!

Without fear, and full of faith, let's continue our adventure. I want to talk to you about the saints in Heaven, otherwise called the 'Cloud of Witnesses'.

If like me, you were brought up in evangelical Church circles you might have been taught the saints are just on vacation all the time, worshipping or enjoying mansions and parks in Heaven!

This is partly true! They are having a brilliant time. As C.S. Lewis rightly said:

Joy is the serious business of Heaven![1]

Heaven is a very happy place! God sits in Heaven and laughs (Psalms 2:4). The angels throw parties (Luke 15:10). They all gather in a big festive assembly (Heb 12:22). It's pretty wild!

However, there are many in Heaven who do have responsibilities. Some are even sitting on thrones. They are reigning now with Christ.

He who overcomes (is victorious), I will grant him to sit beside Me on My throne, as I Myself overcame (was victorious) and sat down beside My Father on His throne (Rev 3:21, AMPC).

Rick Joyner, from Morningstar Ministries, was taken up into Heaven and saw this first hand. In his ground breaking book *The Final Quest*, Rick writes:

As I approached the Judgment seat of Christ, those in the highest ranks were also sitting on thrones that were all a part of His throne. Even the least of these thrones was more glorious than any earthly throne many times over. Some of these were rulers over the affairs of Heaven, and others over the affairs of the physical creation, such as star systems and galaxies.[2]

Jesus himself is the Pattern for this, even now in Heaven. He shows us how we should live as mature sons.

Jesus Christ the faithful *and* trustworthy Witness, the Firstborn of the dead [first to be brought back to life] and the Prince (Ruler) of the kings of the earth (Rev 1:5, AMPC).

Jesus is the ultimate witness. He finished the course. He completed the work of the Father and stands forever in the eternal Order of Melchizedek (Heb 7:17).

Now, let me ask you a question. I want you to think about this, because it's important. Is Jesus just enjoying Heaven now and doing nothing but celebrating?

The obvious answer is no! Scripture says He is interceding (Heb 7:25), reigning (1 Cor 15:25), revealing (Rev 1:11), preparing (John 14:2), leading (Col 1:18) and standing against the enemy (Rev 12:10). He is alive and very active!

If that is the case for Jesus, and he is the Model of us, why then does the Church seem to think that the overcoming saints are just playing games or having picnics in Heaven? It is bizarre! We have this weird idea Heaven is an epic retirement club.

I have found the opposite is true. The faithful saints are fully involved in the government of Heaven, completing the acts written in the 'Books of Destiny' (Psalms 139:16). They are the Ecclesia in Heaven, working with the Ecclesia of Earth, together as one family.

I bow my knees to the Father of our Lord Jesus Christ, from whom the whole family in heaven AND earth is named (Eph 3:14).

That in the dispensation of the fullness of the times He might gather together in ONE all things in Christ, both which are in heaven AND which are on earth - in Him (Eph 1:10).

They are not retired, only translated into another dimension with a different kind of body, working closely with us, still fully alive and engaged with the cosmos. In union with God they draw near and surround us, right now cheering us on.

Hebrews 12:1 says:

a large crowd of witnesses is all around us! (CEV)
huge crowd of men of faith watching us (TLB)
we stand surrounded (VOI)
encircling us (RHM)
on every side (TCNT)
vast crowd of spectators (WMS)

The idea contained in this verse is that they are very close. We are in their atmosphere. As close as your hand held against your face. All distance has been cancelled at the cross. We are One!

American author Roberts Liardon saw the witnesses as a very young boy. He was taken out of his bedroom up into Heaven by Jesus. Roberts wrote about it in a book called *We saw Heaven*. He said:

We passed something I had never expected to see in Heaven which struck me at the time as the funniest thing I had seen. Yet,

when I considered it later, it was one of the most moving and encouraging sights of my Christian walk with God... I saw the great cloud of witnesses.

They are aware of what the church is doing spiritually. When I am preaching for example, they are cheering me on, yelling, "Do this... do that... go!" When "halftime" comes, every one of them hits their knees and begins to pray. Halftime is prayer time. Then they get back up and start cheering again. It is as though we are in a big game, one that is serious and for real - not a game just for fun! And we have some fans cheering us on. They are backing us 100% percent saying "Go! Go get 'em! That's right, Go!"

If we clearly understood the scripture about there being one family in heaven and on earth, we would hear in our spirits what our family in Heaven is saying. If we could hear that "cloud of witnesses," we would be successful in every area of our lives.[3]

This is what Jesus wants us to see right now. We may be in dark times but we are surrounded by allies. In this "KAINOS" era the thin illusionary membrane between us and them is dissolving.

Again, Jesus' life on Earth testified to us what this dynamic relationship should look like. On the mountain, Elijah and Moses, two of the great heroes, appeared to cheer him on.

Suddenly there at the top of the mountain were Moses and Elijah, *those icons of the faith, beloved of God.* **And they talked to Jesus (Mat 17:3, VOI).**

The Message Translation says "They were in deep conversation." I love that!

Don't you want that? I've met the saints many times. Each encounter changed my life.

I have even found they are connected to us on a level we don't yet understand. The truth is we need the whole Church to work together as one mystical body. We cannot finish this cosmic assignment alone. **Having obtained a good testimony through faith, did not receive the promise, God having prepared something better for us, that they should not be made perfect apart from us (Heb 11:39-40).**

It is only together that we will see the Earth transformed. This is all God's idea.

I am convinced the appearance of the saints is going to intensify. There are hints to what is coming in Matthew 27:50-53. It is an astonishing story that is almost hard to believe!

And Jesus cried out again with a loud voice, and yielded up His spirit. Then, behold, the veil of the temple was torn in two from top to bottom; and the earth quaked, and the rocks were split, and the graves were opened; and many bodies of the saints who had fallen asleep were raised; and coming out of the graves after His resurrection, they went into the holy city and appeared to many.

Did you read that? The saints came into the holy city! They actually walked around town with new bodies. Isn't that something?! That is how unified we have become at the cross. That is the power of Life revealed in the Gospel - the 'Glad Message'.

As UK singer Godfrey Birtill says:

Two thousand years ago, we bled into one, every distance has been cancelled in Christ and separation is an illusion, a lie.[4]

I love the following definition of Church, jointly agreed by Catholics and Evangelicals:

The Church is the people of God, the body and the bride of Christ, and the temple of the Holy Spirit. The one, universal Church is a transnational, transcultural, transdenominational, and multi-ethnic family, the household of faith. In the widest sense, the Church includes all the redeemed of all the ages, being the one body of Christ extended throughout time as well as space.[5]

Following on from the cross, the saints have continued throughout the ages to appear to many Christians both in visits to Heaven and also appearances on the Earth. In fact Acts records a really amusing story about two men appearing ('men in white' - always a give away in Scripture!). Check this out:

As He (Jesus) finished this commission, He began to rise from the ground before their eyes until the clouds obscured Him from their vision. As they strained to get one last glimpse of Him going into heaven, the Lord's (apostles) realized two men in white robes were standing among them. *Two Men: You Galileans, why are you standing here staring up into the sky? This Jesus who is leaving you and ascending to heaven will return in the same way you see Him departing* (Acts 1:9-11, VOI).

Hilarious! I find that story very funny! Two saints were given a mission on Earth (what Bill Johnson calls "Shore leave") to ask them why they are looking up?! Isn't it obvious?! Jesus just blew their minds levitating and vanishing. I've realised comedy was God's idea! You've got to have a sense of play and joy to be around Him. He's the blissfully happy God (1 Tim 1:11).

After the time of the book of Acts, the heavenly saints have continued to appear on Earth throughout the ages. The history books are crammed full of stories of them coming to teach, comfort and at times even help. They often appear when someone is dying. They come to honour their lives and accompany them into Heaven. I could pick so many stories, however since space is short I'll give you one of my favourites.

It is taken from the life of Joseph of Copertino.[6] Joseph was praying in the church at night and a demonic being came in the room to try and intimidate him by blowing out the candles. Check out what happens next!

The infernal [demonic] spirits treated Joseph as their enemy. One night the servant of God was standing before the altar of St. Francis, in the Basilica at Assisi, when he heard the door open

violently and saw a man enter, who advanced so noisily that his feet seemed cased in iron. The saint regarded him closely and saw that, as he approached, the lamps went out, one by one, till finally all were extinguished and the intruder stood at his side in utter darkness.

Imagine that! You're in the dark with this evil being standing in front of you. Very creepy!

Thereupon the devil, for he it was, furiously attacked Joseph, threw him on the floor, and attempted to strangle him. Joseph however, invoked [called for] St. Francis, and saw him come forth from his tomb and relight with a small candle all the lamps, at the gleam of which the fiend suddenly vanished. By reason of this occurrence Joseph gave St. Francis the name "Lamplighter of the Church".

Isn't that amazing! I believe it. St. Francis once said:

All the darkness in the world cannot extinguish the light of a single candle.[7]

He was right and saw this fulfilled even after his death. The candle still burned.

If you can see the future, you can be a part of the future. The saints saw our day by faith. The 'Cloud of Witnesses' live with us in their hearts, loving us like grandparents. Permitted to encourage us as the Spirit leads, they are intimately connected to our lives, not being complete apart from us (Heb 11:39-40). They want us to succeed with them.

Would you like to experience more of this community in your own life? I'm sure you would. We should never feel alone.

Paul Keith Davis (White Dove Ministries), has found the connection between honouring the saints and manifestation:

I am convinced what you talk about comes. If you talk about angels

they come. If you talk about the champions of the faith they come. If you talk about what they did and the mantles they carried and contending for it in this generation then what you are saying will come into the room. We are being watched! You are being watched.[8]

This is really how it started for me - I read books on the lives of the saints, contemplating and meditating on how the Lord moved through them, praying and engaging Heaven by faith. I eventually found the Lord introduced me to his dear friends.

One of the most recent was in September 2015. Quite unexpectedly, the French mystic Madame Guyon came in the Spirit to our home. She humbly kneeled before me, silently praying. The Presence of God rushed through the whole house. My wife Rachel came downstairs to see what was happening. It was precious and life changing.

Don't you want your own experiences like this? Then live with an open heart.

There is something about a posture of honour and desire, that attracts the substance of Heaven. It's that simple. Life flows through honour.

The truth is you are not alone. You will never be alone.

All illusions of distance have been fully cancelled in Jesus.

We are One.

TELEPATHIC BY DESIGN

Jesus knew their thoughts (Mat 12:25).

In the next two chapters we are going to build on our "KAINOS" world by looking at a new way we can communicate in the Spirit. A priceless ability that activates more fully as we mature with Christ. The media calls this ability 'telepathy'. Scientists sometimes call it 'mental radio'.

Don't get freaked out! I know how challenging and controversial this may sound. Please stick with me. You will not only be reassured that it is entirely biblical but you will see it is something Jesus did every day.

You will also be excited at the possibilities that await you as a "KAINOS" being. Just like Jesus, you are destined to become increasingly telepathic. It is NATURAL in the new creation order of life. It is the future.

Dictionary.com defines telepathy as -

The communication between people of thoughts, feelings, desires, etc., involving mechanisms that cannot be understood in terms of known scientific laws.

The word "tele" simply means "over a distance" (like tele-vision). Whilst "pathy" means perception or empathy. Catholic theologians have a word for this. They call it "cardio-gnosis" which means "heart to heart knowledge". Isn't that beautiful?

In 1930, a man called Upton Sinclair wrote a famous book about this called *Mental Radio*. He proposed telepathy was a scientific phenomena. Upton based it on many interesting experiments with his wife and close friends. Albert Einstein endorsed this unusual pioneering book and said the idea was worth exploring:

(Mental radio) deserves the most earnest consideration, not only of the laity, but also of the psychologist by profession.[1]

Despite not fully understanding what was happening, Sinclair and Einstein both believed there was something hidden going on. Something science doesn't understand... yet!

In 1924, another scientist Hans Berge also witnessed telepathy in action. He had a dangerous horse accident and nearly died. Somehow his sister sensed it happen.

Hans Berger, the German who recorded the first human electroencephalogram (EEG) in 1924... fell while riding a horse and was almost run over by a team of horses racing down the road inches from his head. His sister, many miles away, sensed the danger and insisted that her father send a telegram to find out what was wrong. She had never sent a telegram before, and the experience left Burger so curious that he switched from studying math and astronomy to medicine hoping to discover the source of that psychic energy.[2]

Have you ever had something like that? You knew something was wrong with a friend. You don't know how. You just knew.

Years ago, I remember a strong urge to phone my friend Mary. Something was seriously up! I called Mary immediately. It turned out she had a very nasty situation that day at work. She lived alone and the call timing was perfect.

It's strange, but we all do this. We think of a friend, then they suddenly message us on Facebook or call. How does that happen? We burst into song and someone else says "I was just thinking of that song!" We meet a person for the first time and something doesn't feel right. How did you know they couldn't be trusted?

Or have you noticed two people often have the same idea at the same time? How many times do two new movies, or two technologies come out that are nearly identical? In fact it is so common scientists have a specific name for this, they call it the "multiples effect":

There is a fascinating phenomenon in science known as the "multiples effect". The multiples effect is when multiple people geographically isolated from one another come up with the exact same discovery at the exact same time. People who have absolutely no communication with one another come upon the exact same discoveries and inventions at the same time, often not realizing that their idea has already been recently presented to the public by someone working on the same problem.[3]

The evidence is growing that people can connect outside of the current paradigm of physics. In 2014, scientists broke the news they had successfully sent a mental message:

Scientists have sent a 'mental message' from one person to another 4,000 miles away in what they claim is the world's first successful telepathy experiment. They connected one person in Mumbai, India, to a wireless headset linked to the internet, and another person to a similar device in Paris. When the first person merely thought of a greeting such as 'ciao', Italian for 'hello', the recipient in France was aware of the thought occurring.[4]

I've included the science to get you thinking.

The more important question for us is, what does the Bible say? Was Jesus telepathic? Can we see it in Scripture? The simple answer is "Yes"! Absolutely! It is throughout the Bible. It was NORMAL for Christ to hear the hidden inner thoughts. Check out the following verses with innocent new creation eyes. It's incredible!

But He, knowing their thoughts, said to them (Luke 11:17-18).

Jesus, knowing their thoughts, said,
"Why do you think evil in your hearts?" (Mat 9:3-5).

But Jesus knew their thoughts, and said to them (Mat 12:25).

Jesus cut to the core of the real inner heart issue. Targeting the secret motives of the soul. He often answered not their spoken words, but their secret and deepest longings, the true questions. In Heaven, the heart speaks louder than the tongue.

Jesus knew what was in their hearts (John 2:24, DAR).

I know everyone's thoughts and feelings (Rev 2:23, CEV).

I X-ray every motive (Rev 2:23, MSG).

This one is one of my favourites:

But Jesus didn't entrust his life to them. He knew them inside and out, knew how untrustworthy they were. He didn't need any help in seeing right through them (John 2:24, MSG).

He saw right through them! Oh boy do we need that today!

Jesus came as Light and Truth. He was functioning free from external illusions. Nobody could fool him with their nice appearance, titles or educated words. He would not play the human mind-games and trade into lies. Facebook and Twitter wouldn't impress!

For the Lord searches all hearts and minds, and understands every intent and inclination of the thoughts (1 Chron 28:9, AMP) ...for as he thinks in his heart, so is he (Prov 23:7).

Yet in it all, God saw through the lens of Love. He saw the hidden treasure. Pulled the people out of illusion and mental prisons, awakening the lost. Drawing them back into the real world.

Jesus didn't use telepathy to condemn humanity. He came to show us God is for us. He came to bring justice for the needy and freedom for the captives.

He [Jesus] won't judge by appearances, won't decide on the basis of hearsay. He'll judge the needy by what is right, render decisions on Earth's poor with justice. (Is 11:3, MSG).

Cardio-gnosis or telepathy is not about condemnation or treating people badly. It is simply about living from a higher perspective. It is the joy of knowing and being known. Being vulnerable and honest with one another. Walking in the Light in true community.

Can you imagine Jesus without this ability? I can't.

Then why do you imagine yourself without this ability?

The exact life in Christ is now repeated in us. We are being co-revealed in the same bliss; we are joined in oneness with him, just as his life reveals you, your life reveals Him! (Col 3:4, MIR).

For He is the Mirror of you!

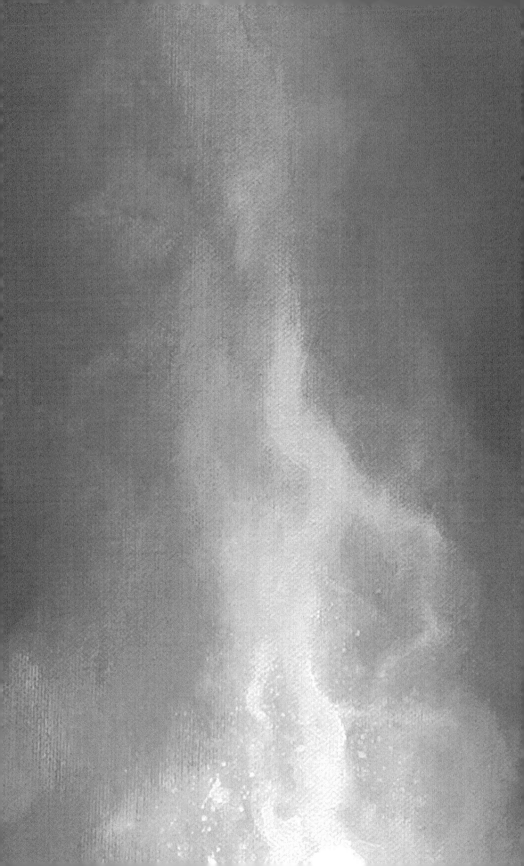

TELEPATHIC HUBS: ONE BODY

Each one of us is joined with one another, and we become together what we could not be alone (Rom 12:5, VOI).

You're still with me? You survived hearing the word TELEPATHY in the last chapter and you're still hungry to know more. That's great! There's so much more to know!

This will continue until we are united by our faith and by our understanding of the Son of God. Then we will be mature, just as Christ is, and we will be completely like him (Eph 4:13, CEV).

We want to be fully formed in Christ, all grown up, fully alive and fully revealed!

In this chapter we're going to expand on the last one by sharing stories from the saints and by talking about how telepathy works in our lives today. I then want to show you that it is possible for entire communities to function this way. In fact it is going to happen!

Don't be offended by this. It's just the way we were made. It is the way we were always meant to be before the fall. The Ethiopic book of Enoch[1] records that people were not supposed to rely on books to pass on knowledge. Books don't require intimacy. You can read a biography without ever meeting a person. Originally, we were meant to live forever and impart knowledge through direct connection. Adam was meant to be a living book, wide open, full of light, imparting to generation upon generation through cardio-gnosis.

This is coming again. It is our future. We see glimpses of this in the past lives of the saints. In this next remarkable story, French mystic Jeanne Guyon found she could communicate heart to heart, during a period of serious illness.

During this extraordinary sickness, the Lord gradually showed me another way for souls to converse - in profound silence. Whenever Father La Combe entered the room, I would speak to him only in silence. Our hearts spoke to each other, communicating grace without words. It was like going to a new country, both for him and for me, but it was obviously so divine, I cannot describe it. We passed many hours in this silence, always communicative, without uttering one word... I was later able to communicate in this way with other souls, but it was one-way communication. I imparted grace to them but received nothing from them. With Father La Combe, there was a back and forth communication of grace.²

Beautiful! This is true unity, Oneness, the way it is meant to be. Don't you want that?!

St. Gerard Majella is another Saint who read people's hearts and knew exactly what was going on with them. This is an amusing story of him catching a fake disabled beggar!

(He) detested the practise of some men who pretended to be crippled in order to live on the charity of others. On one occasion the Saint saw a man dragging himself along on his crutches, one leg bandaged in old rags, pleading for alms... Gerard approached the man, tore off his bandages and ordered the man to stop the pretence for the good of his soul. "Beholding his fraud discovered, the pretended cripple ran off on both legs, forgetful of even his crutches."³

This ability was particularly useful in confession times! Ha!

(St. Philip Neri) also had the gift of reading souls and hearts. This gift was exercised frequently in the confessional when a sin had been forgotten or a penitent withheld the telling of a grievous

sin out of shame. One time, when a young man found it difficult to describe a certain sin, the Saint had pity on him and revealed exactly how it had taken place.[4]

We need this today. Aren't you tired of us being duped by false people, whether politicians, celebrities or Youtube ministries? With the internet we need discernment every day!

The truth is, I can't imagine living without this now. I have found cardio-gnosis is essential as I have travelled around the world. It really isn't optional if we want to disciple nations.

I remember the first time my wife and I heard someone's thoughts together. We were on the beach in Wales setting up our sun-tent. There was a woman sitting further behind us. Together, my wife and I heard her thinking "I don't want them there, they are blocking the view of the sea." We turned to each other and said "Did you hear that?!" We found it amusing God would allow us to hear this... and of course we moved our tent much further away up the beach!

I have put such a value on this ability. I can't function without it. Often when I travel, I see how much spiritual authority is on the leader. I can tell if a person is struggling and at times what the issues are. I can sense their destiny scroll and whether they are in alignment. Often I can sense if they are lying.

Once in Spirit School, a young man talked to me about purity. Sadly, he wasn't being honest with me. In his thoughts I could see he had slept with a girl that week. He also had other drug related problems too. I smiled and hugged him. I didn't expose him. I just understood where he was coming from. He needed Papa. He needed love.

I have found telepathy is much stronger in deeper states of union. When I'm absorbed in the presence, sometimes in a flash I can see what people are really like. It seems like I've known them for years. It doesn't happen all the time, but I really like it when it does.

I've also experienced cardio-gnosis on a big scale. During worship at a large conference my chest filled with a warm honey-like presence. My heart was swelling with God's love. The thoughts and feelings of everyone in the room pressed in on me. It was unusual.

When my mind is still and deeply absorbed in the Lord, I occasionally hear people's questions before they ask them. More often with very close friends. When you hold someone in your heart it seems easier to connect. I sometimes forget to wait for them to speak before answering. It has made us laugh a number of times!

Don't get freaked out by this. Be open. As I've shown you already in the previous chapter, it is deeply biblical. Let's look at another example from Acts:

Then Peter said, "Ananias, how is it that Satan has so filled your heart that you have lied to the Holy Spirit and have kept for yourself some of the money you received for the land? ...How is it that you have agreed together to test the Spirit of the Lord?" (Acts 5:5-9).

Peter saw right through them. Incredible! We know the rest of the story. They suddenly died. Can you imagine that? Shocking isn't it!

Yet imagine if Peter had not seen. The entire church would have partnered with deceit and mockery. Traded into Satan's platform of greed and pride, agreed with corruption.

We need to come back to this level of insight. We cannot fudge this vital subject any longer. We cannot be moved by the seen. Paul knew the outside was not reality. It's the inside that counts.

We do not know anyone in a purely human way (2 Cor 5:16, HCSB) From a human point of view (LEB).

We have to see beyond skin and beyond negative and positive rumours, just like God:

For man looks at the outward appearance, but the Lord looks at

the heart. (1 Sam 16:7).

This is exactly how things work now in Heaven. In that higher unseen dimension, our thoughts speak louder than words. We communicate colours, frequency and sound.

I have seen the saints TRANSFIGURED in the Council of God. Speaking to each other in high-speed beams of living colours, just like spiritual fibre optics. Captivating streams of pinks, peaches, blues, yellows flowing spirit to spirit through the air. All interacting together like a living hive mind. Speaking faster than I can comprehend. It's captivating. Immense beauty.

We see a lower form of this direct messaging in the Bible. Paul had a man appear in a vision from Macedonia. He spoke to Paul in the telepathic realm of communication.

And a vision appeared to Paul in the night. A man of Macedonia stood and pleaded with him, saying, "Come over to Macedonia and help us." (Acts 16:9).

Some call this "Dream Invasion". It was common in the lives of the saints in history. Ian Clayton amusingly calls this "Spirit text-messaging". He does it a lot!

Taking community up another level, Paul, the radical mystic saw it was possible for us on Earth to be synchronised as a community spiritual-hub. Just like my visits to Heaven:

Complete my joy by living in harmony and being of the same mind and one in purpose, having the same love, being in full accord and of one harmonious mind and intention (Phil 2:2, AMP).

Or more simply **...be of ONE MIND (2 Cor 13:11).**

This is "KAINOS" spiritual technology. We are a living communication hub that transcends the space-time matrix. Every definition of distance has been cancelled in Christ. We are mystically entangled together in

Love, in the communion of One Body.

I have found the deeper we enjoy union and the more we engage the presence of God, the deeper this ability operates. The more clothed I am in the Divine Essence, the more natural this new blissful world becomes. Of myself I can do nothing. It is in union we reach perfection.

Disconnection is simply the false perception of our minds. Reality is Oneness.

We are many people, but in Christ we are all one body. We are the parts of that body, and each part belongs to all the others (Rom 12:5, ERV).

Each one of us is joined with one another, and we become together what we could not be alone (Rom 12:5, VOI).

"We become TOGETHER what we could not be alone" I love that.

The future will be defined by Oneness.

REMOTESIGHT

Before Christ, humanity was severely limited to the physical world. We were bound by space and time. Stuck to the confines of our natural bodies. Spiritually blind. Fallen.

In the new creation, this all changed. The fruit of being born-again is sight. Faith opens our eyes.

For we are looking all the time not at the visible things but at the invisible. The visible things are transitory: it is the invisible things that are really permanent (2 Cor 4:18, PHI).

The Apostle Paul thought it was natural to see. He encouraged his followers to look at the invisible, to always set their sight on things Above. Paul was a mystic!

Look up, and be alert to what is going on around Christ - that's where the action is (Col 3:1, MSG).

This is another mystery of the Gospel. It is modelled for us by John the Beloved. He was in the Spirit on the Lord's day. He heard a voice and "turned to see" (see Rev 1). When we are in the Spirit we can "turn to see" as God wills. I have found he longs to show us his world. He wants us to see.

World governments are aware that humans (even in their fallen state) have some ability to see distant events. Like telepathy, this is beyond the current understanding of science. Yet they know something is going on. They call this ability "Remote Viewing".

Remote viewing (RV) is the practice of seeking impressions about a distant or unseen target using subjective means, in particular, extrasensory perception (ESP) or "sensing with mind."[1]

The USA developed a project to explore this. They called it "Project Stargate". It sounds like science fiction I know! But it's true! It officially ran for 20 years until 1995. The 'official line' is that it was a failure. However, if you dig around the evidence you will find some people were very skilled at it. One man was able to identify features of the Solar System before NASA got there with satellites. Something is going on!

If then, the natural man can access some of this ability - how much more can we, the "KAINOS" sons who are infused and joined with the Divine Nature, be able to see?

Forerunner Nancy Coen calls this new creation ability "Unlimited Vision".

It's amazing. Such a gift! Even the amazing Hubble telescope can't compare to the range of our vision. Have you looked at the cosmos with Jesus?

As this age ends and another begins, we will find clarity of vision. We will come of age.

But solid food belongs to those who are of full age, *that is*, those who by reason of use have their senses exercised (Heb 5:14).

What was once just for prophets will be normal for all. Let's look at some examples:

Would you like to protect your nation from attack? This is exactly what Elisha did for Israel. Whenever the King of Syria invaded, Israel was ready for him and won the fight. They were tipped off! The King was furious. Was there a spy in the camp?

Therefore the heart of the king of Syria was greatly troubled by this thing; and he called his servants and said to them, "Will you not show me which of us *is* for the king of Israel?"

And one of his servants said, "None, my lord, O king; but Elisha, the prophet who *is* in Israel, tells the king of Israel the words that you speak in your bedroom." (2 Kings 6:11-12).

Elisha had learned the mystery I'm teaching you right now. He was a shield to his nation and protected it from evil. He helped the government. He was living beyond the limitations of locality. He'd learned how to move in the Kingdom Realm with God.

What about seeing secret meetings? Would you like to know what is going on around the Globe? The prophet Ezekiel saw the secret idolatry behind closed doors and who was involved. He was aware of government corruption and the cabals of his generation.

And He said to me, "Go in, and see the wicked abominations which they are doing there." So I went in and saw, and there - every sort of creeping thing, abominable beasts, and all the idols of the house of Israel, portrayed all around on the walls. And there stood before them seventy men of the elders of the house of Israel, and in their midst stood Jaazaniah the son of Shaphan. Each man had a censer in his hand, and a thick cloud of incense went up. Then He said to me, "Son of man, have you seen what the elders of the house of Israel do in the dark, every man in the room of his idols? For they say, 'The Lord does not see us, the Lord has forsaken the land.'" (Ez 8:9-12).

These evil people believed they could get away with it because the Lord does not see! How true is this today? How many governments and corporations are undertaking unethical deals right now? They think it is hidden. This too is going to change!

Therefore do not fear them. For there is nothing covered that will not be revealed, and hidden that will not be known (Mat 10:26).

I believe new Ecclesia hubs are going to appear in every nation that will see, hear and understand. They will be infused with knowledge and shine with Wisdom.

There are small hints in the past showing what is to come, especially with the Celtic saints. In an era without cell phones or "Facebook" they relied on "Unlimited Vision" and cardio-gnosis to stay connected. They knew what was going on.

One day, on Iona, St. Columba suddenly got up from his reading and said with a smile: "Now I must hurry to the church to beseech God on behalf of a poor girl who is tortured by the pains of a most difficult childbirth and who now in Ireland calls on my name. For she hopes that through me the Lord will release her from her anguish, because she is related to me, for her father belonged to my mother's kindred."[2]

Notice she called for him. She made contact spirit to spirit through cardio-gnosis. A spirit-text message to find help. When your heart moves your spirit follows. If the other person is open and aware they will sense you and respond back. It's a spirit-phone call.

Columba's story continues:

St Columba was moved by pity for the girl and ran to the church where he knelt and prayed to Christ the Son of Man. Then after praying he came out and said to those of the brethren who met him: "Now has our Lord Jesus, who was born of a woman, shown favour on the poor girl and brought timely help to deliver her from her difficulties. She has safely given birth and is in no danger of death."

They later found from local people, all Columba had said was true. This was normal for Columba. The prophetic operated with clarity and accuracy. Something we will see again as the new oracles emerge across the Earth. People like Samuel who's words will not fall to the ground. A higher prophetic ministry is coming.

In the next story, Columba met a man at a guest house. Immediately, he saw where the man was from, and saw key events taking place with his family back home.

When the Saint saw him, he said: "Where do you live?"
"In Cruach Rannoch near the shore of the loch."
"That district you name," said the Saint, "is where savage marauders are now plundering." The poor layman, hearing this, began to grieve for his wife and children, but the saint comforted him in his sorrow, saying: "Go, dear fellow, go. Your whole family has fled up the mountainside and escaped, though the cruel raiders have driven away with them your little herd, and have taken as booty the furniture of your house." When the layman returned to his own district, he found that everything he had heard the saint say was fulfilled.

The late prophet Bob Jones would frequently have experiences like this. Some of the stories are hilarious! I remember years ago hosting Jeff Jansen (Global Fire Ministries) in Wales for a conference. Jeff was resting back in the hotel. He looked in the mirror and suddenly saw Bob (who was one of his mentors) standing behind him. Shocked, Jeff turned around and saw he was still alone. Jeff immediately called Bob in America to see if it was really him. Bob laughed and said "Yep, I was checking in on my boys!" He loved Jeff and was making sure he was doing okay on his trip to Wales. I love that! That is "KAINOS" living!

I have learned from the Lord that if you hold someone in your heart - if you love them and keep them inside your spirit like a treasure - then you will see and feel more about their lives. Your spirit will follow your heart (see 2 Kings 5:26).

I have seen distant events. I have witnessed in dreams and visions board meetings and conversations in other places. I once saw what my wife Rachel was doing in the kitchen when I was in the living room. Sometimes I've even been permitted to see off-world into space.

Our Elder-brother is the Prototype. He is the Rock on which we stand and base our lives. Jesus lived free from human limitations and could see beyond his natural eyes.

Jesus saw Nathanael coming toward Him, and said of him, "Behold, an Israelite indeed, in whom is no deceit!" Nathanael said to Him, "How do You know me?" Jesus answered and said to him, "Before Philip called you, when you were under the fig tree, I saw you." (John 1:47).

He saw Nathanael before they even met. This specific word about the fig tree cut Nathanael to the heart. Immediately he believed.

Has this ever happened to you? Have you ever met someone and felt you already knew them? Perhaps you did see them previously in the Spirit. You would be surprised how active your spirit-being actually is. It is always moving, especially at night. It never sleeps.

Our vision is not limited even to people or the nations. Yes we can see distant events here, like Elisha seeing the King of Syria, but we can also see the heavenly. Jesus said:

I was watching and saw Satan fall from heaven like a flash of lightning! (Luke 10:17-20, PHI).

He was always seeing through multiple dimensions, working with his Father. In fact, to truly function as a mature son, we must see.

Then Jesus answered and said to them, "Most assuredly, I say to you, the Son can do nothing of Himself, but what He sees the Father do; for whatever He does, the Son also does in like manner" (John 5:19)... "I speak what I have seen with My Father" (John 8:38).

The whole world is wide-open to His sight.

The Lord's eyes keep on roaming throughout the earth (2 Chron 16:9, ISV).

Where can I go from Your Spirit? Or where can I flee from Your presence? If I ascend into heaven, You are there; if I make my bed in hell, behold, You are there. If I take the wings of the morning, and dwell in the uttermost parts of the sea, even there Your hand shall lead me, and Your right hand shall hold me (Psalms 139:7).

The Psalmist understood God's Spirit was everywhere and that he filled everything - even hell. Creation is smaller than the Trinity. Even the heavens of heavens is too small.

Heaven and the heaven of heavens cannot contain You (1 Kings 8:27).

(Jesus) who came down is the same one who went up higher than all the heavens. He did this so that he would be everywhere (Eph 4:10, WE).

I love this. These verses are gold. Doorways into the Divine Ocean! Jump in!

This is where it also gets amazing for us as sons. Aren't we also joined to his Spirit now? Isn't the Gospel a message of union with him? A spiritual marriage? Yes!

But the one who joins himself with the Lord becomes ONE spirit with him (1 Cor 6:17, WE).

Then in some new mystical way, we can access EVERYWHERE in Christ because we are already everywhere in Christ. We are in Him and Christ is in us! Amazing! As Paul said:

God's Spirit beckons. There are things to do and places to go! (Rom 8:14, MSG).

I love that invitation! Like Aladdin in the Disney cartoon, Holy Spirit reaches out and says "Do you trust Me?" Maybe you've not seen that film? The young girl Jasmine thinks about the offer to fly, then jumps on the magic carpet with Aladdin. They begin to sing an amazing song about seeing a 'whole new world' (sound familiar?)![3]

Aladdin sings **"I can open your eyes, take you wonder by wonder..."**

This is a prophetic picture of what moving in the Spirit is like. It's not scary. You are with Him. You are not alone. He takes you. He shows you. It is in Oneness we fly upon grace!

Jasmine sings back to Aladdin:

"I'm like a shooting star, I've come so far I can't go back to where I used to be."

This is Heaven's dream for us. That we go so far out we never go back. Just like Enoch!

INFUSED KNOWLEDGE

God gave Solomon wisdom - the deepest of understanding and the largest of hearts. There was nothing beyond him, nothing he couldn't handle (1 Kings 4:29, MSG).

I'm glad you're still reading! I know it's been stretching for some of you. Well done for progressing this far. Let's get really hungry for more. You were made for this. I am convinced in the future this will all seem basic 101. We are heading into a new age.

Let's expand our definitions of what is possible NOW. The Church has lived too small. In this chapter we're going to enjoy another set of mystical abilities from our union into the Divine. These are called "Infused Knowledge" and "Expanded Hearts".

Like the Tardis in Dr. Who (yes I am a geek!) we are much bigger on the inside than the outside. Inside is stored all the riches and mysteries of Heaven. We just have to learn how to pull from this hidden treasure to help the world. Living inside to out.

Let's begin with "Infused Knowledge". It can be defined as:

The gift of natural (secular) and supernatural (spiritual) knowledge miraculously conferred by God. Thought by some to have been possessed by Adam and Eve, who came into existence in an adult state and were to be the first teachers of the human race.[1]

Infused knowledge is knowledge imparted directly into us by God. It doesn't come through earthly study. It's not natural. It's supernatural!

It is not limited to one subject. It could be knowledge about science, music, language, time, people, art, or even about the Cosmos. It can come suddenly in a flash or gently over time. It is a fruit of mystical union.

I am the Vine, you are the branches. When you're joined with me and I with you, the relation intimate and organic, the harvest is sure to be abundant. Separated, you can't produce a thing (John 15:7, MSG).

The amazing thing about infused knowledge is that it can sometimes come in secret, without you knowing how it got there. It can soak into your heart during the night or in the presence.

For God may speak in one way, or in another,
Yet *man* does not perceive it.
In a dream, in a vision of the night,
When deep sleep falls upon men,
While slumbering on their beds,
Then He opens the ears of men,
And seals their instruction.
(Job 33:14-16).

Years ago I was seriously impacted listening to Joshua Mills (New Wine International). Joshua told us a story about him powerfully encountering God when he was a teenager. He was in a Church meeting and was suddenly intoxicated by the Holy Spirit. The next morning, Joshua woke up able to play the keyboard and write songs. It was all there, he could just do it. God 'sealed the instruction' in him during the night. Don't you want that?! Divine downloading!

Infused knowledge is connected to union. We talk about this often in our Podcasts. It is simply one of the fruits of friendship. One of the defining marks of true spiritual ecstasy.

I once experienced this phenomenon on the plane to do youth meetings in France. I was enjoying the sweetness of God and suddenly I was taken up. In a flash I found myself in Heaven. I saw the 'Books of the Future' and was given understanding about Enoch. I understood the Ecclesia would actually re-build ruined cities, landscape the Earth and transform DNA. I had been infused with Isaiah 61:3-4. Amazing!

Some believe Adam had this type of knowledge, that early humans had 100% brain power. Created ready to go, Adam didn't learn to walk or talk, it was there already. He was born grown up. Adam knew how to work the land and create technology. He was infused with understanding about animals and plants. He knew their nature.

We see this ability often in Jesus. With the woman at the well, Jesus knew her whole life story. Nothing was hidden from him. She was astonished!

And many of the Samaritans of that city believed in Him because of the word of the woman who testified, "He told me all that I *ever* did." (John 4:39).

He knew her inside and out. Knew her history, understood her pain. This wasn't natural knowledge. It was through the Spirit. It came from the Father (1 Cor 2:10).

Have you ever had anything like that? In a flash God downloading something into you?

Church history has many stories like this. I often look to the Celtic saints. They stand as a beacon of light through the ages, marking the British islands with hope. In this story Saint Bridget and her friends were waiting to meet an important official to argue a case.

Bridget loved music and one time at a chieftain's fortress, somewhere near Knockaney (County Limerick), Bridget went to ask for the release of a captive. She was asked to sit and wait for the chieftain by the man's aged foster-father. While she was waiting, she saw some harps hanging on the wall. She asked for some music but the harpists were not there. The sisters with Bridget told the foster-father to take the harp, and while Bridget was present he would be able to play. The old man took down the harp from the wall,

thrummed it clumsily, but suddenly found he could produce airs and harmonies. Another of the household anxiously tried a second harp with the same results. Presently the place was filled with happy music and the chieftain arrived home to hear it. He heard rare laughter from his foster-father. Pleased with his homecoming he conceded to Bridget all that she asked.[2]

Ha! That's a glory invasion! We need more of this today. At work, home, school. Can you see it? I dream of it. I can see the wild islands of Britain resounding with joy!

This miracle was not just limited to ancient times. The American healing evangelist John G. Lake also experienced infused knowledge. Once, John was catching a train and had a strong desire to talk to some Italians waiting at the platform about Jesus.

As I walked up and down the platform I said, "Oh God, how much I would like to be able to talk to these men about the living Christ and His power to save."
The Spirit said, "You can." [3]

Did you hear that? "You can!" God says!

What happened next is pure joy:

I stepped over to them and as I approached them I observed myself commencing to speak in some foreign language. I addressed one of the group and he instantly answered me in Italian. I asked where he was from, and he replied "Naples." For fifteen minutes God let me tell of the truths of Christ and the power of God to that group of labourers in Italian, a language of which I had no knowledge.

John G. Lake prophesied a shower of grace was coming to anoint a future generation to speak EVERY language. He saw what he had was just a flash, a glimpse of what was coming.

Can you imagine that now? All of us speaking MANY languages! The media would stir in wonder. It would shake the world. I dare to believe for such things. As Paul said:

If it seems we are crazy, it is to bring glory to God (2 Cor 5:13, NLT).

The second "KAINOS" power that accompanies this is what I call an "Expanded Heart". It is a profound supernatural capacity to apply knowledge, solve riddles, find solutions.

It is a wise heart beyond natural thinking. It is what Solomon and many saints in history walked in. Read this next verse and imagine it happening to you:

God gave Solomon wisdom - the deepest of understanding and the largest of hearts. There was nothing beyond him, nothing he couldn't handle (MSG).

Elohim **gave Solomon wisdom - keen insight and a mind as limitless as the sand on the seashore (1 Kings 4:29, NOG).**

Wow! I love that... Limitless mind!!

The Bible is full of people who functioned in this ahead of the new creation. Little signs to a bigger day. Daniel was one of them. He took responsibility in the Spirit for a nation and upon that fell authority and an expanded heart.

An extraordinary spirit, knowledge and insight, the ability to interpret dreams, clarify riddles, and solve complex problems were found in this Daniel (Dan 5:12, AMP).

He could do anything - interpret dreams, solve mysteries, explain puzzles (MSG).

Unlock mysteries and solve knotty problems (CJB).

Nothing was beyond Daniel. Nothing... Think about it.

Some believe we use only 10% or less of our brain capacity. What is that extra 90% for? Perhaps the rest is for higher consciousness and dimensional engagement, what we call the spirit realm?

What we do know is that Jesus came to restore all that was lost. Recover all. This includes our intellect and reasoning, our knowledge, the 100% and beyond.

For the Son of Man came to seek and save what was lost (CJB).

The late Bob Jones prophesied we would begin to find our cognitive abilities increased, as we come into the time of the harvest. I believe that.

We simply cannot understand the times we are living in without also understanding there will be a profound increase in revelation, wisdom and understanding.

Your sons will prophesy, also your daughters; your young men will see visions, your old men dream dreams. When the time comes, I'll pour out my Spirit on those who serve me, men and women both, and they'll prophesy (Acts 2:17, MSG).

This is a massive change! We are in the era of Revealed Truth! And it's increasing.

In Enoch's time it was the opposite. Wisdom could find no resting place on Earth. They were a rebellious lawless generation that did not love God. It was a dark time. Wisdom remained locked up in the Heavens. *The Lost Book of Enoch*[4] says:

It seemed strange that wisdom found no place where she might dwell; then a place was assigned to her in the heavens... She went forth to make her dwelling among the children of men but found no dwelling place. She returned to her place and sat among the angels.

Yet Enoch saw a time this would change. A time when people would go into Heaven and drink from the fountains of Wisdom. He saw the emerging Ecclesia communities ahead of time.

I saw the fountain of righteousness, which is inexhaustible. All around were other fountains of wisdom. Those who were thirsty drank of this water and they were filled with wisdom.

Mystic hubs coming up to Zion to learn the ways of God. I love this! It's started.

Enoch then saw Wisdom would saturate the Earth with the secrets of righteousness. A day of knowledge invasion. An outpouring of the Spirit of Wisdom!

Wisdom shall be poured out like water and the glory of God shall never fail. For He is mighty in all things and in all secrets of righteousness.

We are in this time. I believe it. I see it. We have met "KAINOS" people who have been shown new computer technologies, car designs, life extension ideas, cutting edge algorithms, nanotechnology and more. Some of it is wild! It's happening right now, often in secret. I've visited a new creation facility to see some of it for myself. What I saw there was mind-boggling! I loved it!

Don't you want that?

Amazingly God wants this for us also, and even more besides!

It is your Father's good pleasure to give you the kingdom (Luke 12:32).

Doubt nothing! It gives him JOY to share the Kingdom with you!

Call to Me, and I will answer you, and show you great and mighty things, which you do not know (NKJV)... I'll tell you marvellous and wondrous things that you could never figure out on your own (MSG)... things beyond what you can imagine (VOI) (Jer 33:3).

You may feel unqualified to walk like this. The Gospel is the happy message - that you were unqualified - so Jesus did it for you! He lived the perfect life on your behalf. Now we apprehend the Kingdom as a gift, by faith. Believing not achieving!

This grace is coming to little groups scattered all over the globe. Governmental hubs are being birthed again now, in living rooms, in IHOPs (houses of prayer), in Spirit led churches, in the office, in the secret place.

I saw in a dream a housewife being personally mentored by Heaven. As she cleaned she was being taught the secrets of the Kingdom. This continued in secret for years until she was commissioned to teach. One day she stepped out and began to speak. There was no stopping her. She was a new oracle.

For nothing is hidden, except to be revealed; nor has *anything* been secret, but that it would come to light (Mark 4:22).

Governments will come to people like her, invite them to meetings, receive prayer and prophetic ministry from them. They will be essential to resolving the problems of this time. They won't be bought or moved by men, but be moved solely by Heaven, seated in Christ, at rest in the finished work. They will be 'Living Word' ministries.

I chose to talk about this in the firm belief that you are one who has been chosen to know the mysteries. You have been born in a time when Wisdom will pour down like rain. You are going to expand beyond anything you've ever imagined, just like Solomon.

God gave (*your name) - the deepest of understanding and the largest of hearts. There was nothing beyond (*your name), nothing (*your name) couldn't handle (1 Kings 4:29, MSG).

Speak it out. See it. Hunger for it. Dream it. See it. Believe it!

Spy out your inheritance with child-like, innocent "KAINOS" faith.

If you live in Me [abide vitally united to Me] and My words remain in you *and* continue to live in your hearts, ask whatever you will, and it shall be done for you (John 15:7, AMP).

Oneness leads to the words remaining and living in you.

The new oracles are coming ...maybe sooner than we think!

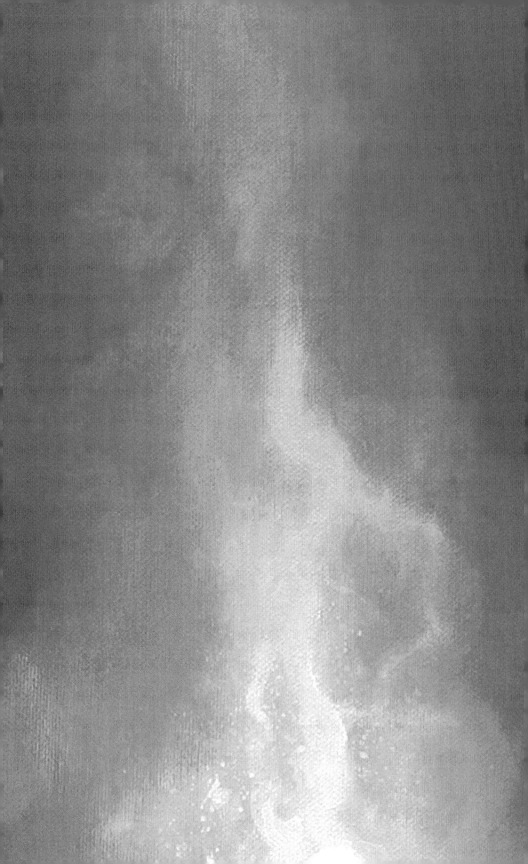

MIRACULOUS
TRANSPORT

"Transportations I believe, are going to be dramatically increasing"
- John Paul Jackson[1]

In 2014, I began to glimpse a mystery. The sons are designed to be able to do things by the Spirit, that natural technology does on the Earth. That technology actually reveals unseen principles. It is a manifestation of the goodness of the Lord.

In the natural world we have seen an astonishing change in the technology of world travel. My Dad told me flying was considered a luxury when he was a kid. It was rare for ordinary people to go abroad. Look back another generation and cars were a luxury item, even further and people travelled in a horse and cart.

One of the developing "KAINOS" technologies is also connected to transport. It is the supernatural ability to teleport from one place to another. I have been shown that some radical people will LIVE in the Spirit, AND they will also MOVE in the Spirit:

For in Him we live and move and have our being (Acts 17:28).

Perhaps Daniel saw this coming. He future gazed and said:

Many will travel everywhere (Dan 12:4, GW).

In fact, I believe as the nations tighten their national borders and we enter into a highly monitored electronic world, it will become essential. The "KAINOS" creation transcends geographic temporal boundaries.

The Earth is the Lord's and everything in it.

Again we gaze lovingly at the Blueprint, to remember who we are and what we do. With a flesh body that could eat and be touched, Jesus instantly transported into the room:

Jesus Himself stood in the midst of them, and said to them, "Peace to you." But they were terrified and frightened, and supposed they had seen a spirit. And He said to them, "Why are you troubled? And why do doubts arise in your hearts? Behold My hands and My feet, that it is I Myself. Handle Me and see, for a spirit does not have flesh and bones as you see I have." (Luke 24:36-39).

This is such an epic story. I wish I was there. I love it.

This wasn't Jesus' only teleportation. On another occasion Jesus instantly shifted the disciples and the fishing boat across the lake. It happened after he walked on water:

But He said to them, "It is I; do not be afraid." Then they willingly received Him into the boat, and IMMEDIATELY the boat was at the land where they were going (John 6:21).

I like how the New Living Translation says it:

Immediately they arrived at their destination! (John 6:21, NLT).

Imagine that happening to you. You get in your car to drive and instantly you're there! The GPS says "You have reached your destination!" Ha! I want that. It would be great to be there instantly.

After Jesus left the Earth, the early church continued to move in this miracle of teleportation. Philip instantly traversed 40 miles in the blink of an eye:

And both Philip and the eunuch went down into the water, and he baptised him. Now when they came up out of the water, the Spirit of the Lord caught Philip away, so that the eunuch saw him

no more; and he went on his way rejoicing. But Philip was found at Azotus. And passing through, he preached in all the cities till he came to Caesarea (Acts 8:38-40).

This ability was normal for some even in the Old Testament. Elijah was frequently moved around Israel by the Spirit. So much so he was asked to stay still for a moment (see 1 Kings 18:12). Elijah had to promise not to vanish. Isn't that something!

This is where we are all going. "KAINOS" life is to move in the Spirit and Power of Elijah!

One of my heroes is the late John Paul Jackson. He honoured me and I will never forget that. John Paul had many unusual experiences. In the following story John Paul shares how a man was transported into his hotel room from Mexico to Switzerland.

I was in Geneva Switzerland. I'd been travelling for 21 days and I was not feeling very good. In fact I was really sick... It wasn't fun. I left Los Angeles airport thinking I would get better... 21 days later I was getting worse.

It was 2:30 in the morning. I am awake hurting really bad, doing my best not to double over in pain. I look at the clock and it says 2:30 and I look to my right and there's this man standing there. I'm sicker than I thought. I think I'm hallucinating. There's nobody here. It's probably an hallucination.

I said, 'Lord if this is you, then I want you to have him touch me and pray for me.. I want him to put his hand on my hand. I don't want the Spirit stuff where it goes right through me. I want to feel the weight of his hand and I want to be healed.'

He's probably late 70s, early 80s, really weathered, he looked like he was Spanish/Mexican. He said, 'I've come to pray for you that you might get well.' He puts his hands on me. Prays for me. It felt like a scroll went into me. It felt thick like honey and as it rolled up there was no pain. It rolled up my head and down my feet and

I was instantly healed. I looked at him and he smiled at me and disappeared right in front of my eyes.

I was healed! I was really happy and got up praising the Lord. I thanked God for sending one of his angels... He said, "It was a servant of Mine from Mexico who lived in a small village and was asking me if there was any way I would use him. So I took him and brought him back."

Telling the story, John Paul laughed and said:

How would you like to be that guy?! I know that is going to happen![2]

I want that. I think we are ready for adventure. It's in our DNA!

My good friend Matthew Nagy (Glory Company) would frequently be transported up one flight of stairs in the morning on his way up to his office. It always took Matt by surprise. He was simply enjoying the sweetness of Jesus, then suddenly up he went! Sounds good to me!

I like shortcuts! My friends John and Ruth Filler came to hear me speak in Oregon USA. It took three hours for them to get to the meeting. The way back took only half the time, despite driving at normal speeds. Isn't that amazing? I call this strange phenomena "rich time" (see Eph 5:16).

Many people email and message us with nearly the exact same stories. This "KAINOS" enablement to shape time and reality is increasing. Strangely, some have even left their home late and still arrived early at the meetings. It's crazy! It's weird! It's so much fun!

I was once on a few days vacation with Ian Clayton and some friends in beautiful New Zealand. We had just visited the famous volcanic pools. Ian was driving us on winding country roads. We were at the top of a mountain looking down into the valley. Within a moment we were at the bottom track. We laughed about it! I would have enjoyed it more had I not been scared of Ian's driving - it was nuts (true story)!

History shows us God is willing to give his friends a helping hand on the journey. He rewards friendship. One of the early Church accounts is that of St. Ammon. The Saint was travelling with his disciple Theodore:

When they reached a stream they had planned to cross, they saw the water had risen and overflowed the banks. They realised they had to swim across instead of walk. The two separated to undress, but St. Ammon, being too shy to swim across naked, was trying to make up his mind what to do when suddenly he was transported to the other side. Theodore, coming up and seeing that he had crossed without getting wet, pressed the Saint for an explanation and was so insistent the Saint finally confessed the miracle.[3]

I think TV wild man Bear Grylls would like to have that miracle!

It seems desire is a powerful force in framing up spiritual possibilities. Expectation produces faith. Faith produces evidence of the unseen. Faith shapes reality.

In this next story St. Dominic wanted to spend the whole night in prayer at the church but it was sadly locked for the evening.

(St. Dominic) was travelling one evening in the company of a Cistercian monk when they approached a neighbouring church. According to the Saint's custom, he wanted to spend the night in prayer before the altar, but was disappointed on finding the church tightly locked for the night. Both decided to spend the night in prayer on the church steps when suddenly, "without being able to say how, they found themselves before the high altar inside the church, and remained there until break of day."[4]

That's the power of desire. It pulls favour from the Father. Notice they also had the ability not to need sleep, a common fruit of mystic union. There is Life in Union.

I recently had the pleasure of hearing Paul Keith Davis sharing stories about the prophet Bob Jones, a personal hero of mine. I wish I had known him on the Earth.

Paul Keith told us how they were at Moravian Falls in the USA. They were there praying for the land to be sold to the church. Early one morning an angel shook Bob awake. He told him to get dressed and come with him. The angel transported Bob up to the top of the hill to confront a demonic being blocking the sale. Bob dealt with it. It's a wild story.

Paul Keith was astonished to wake up early and see Bob slowly walking back down the hill on his own. Bob was waiting for a knee operation at the time and Paul Keith was surprised to see him walking down the hill. Bob told him what happened.

After hearing the whole angel story, Paul Keith pressed Bob to wake him up if an angel ever did that again. Paul Keith laughed telling us the story, but I think he was gutted he missed out on the fun!

Pere Lamy, was another elderly man (like Bob) who was transported to save his poor knees. He was a Catholic parish priest who worked many wonders. He walked closely with the angels and was often helped by them:

I have been upheld by the holy angels many a time, when I have been exhausted with weariness, and have been brought from one place to another without knowing anything about it. I used to say "My God, how tired I am." I was in my parish far away, often at night, and I found myself at the Place St. Lucian all at once. How it happened I don't know.[5]

I love that. Heaven cares!

Ian Clayton is a forerunner in this spiritual technology. Ian has teleportation experiences on a regular basis, appearing in a prison cell to heal a Christian, transporting to China to teach about the Kingdom Realm, saving a family in the Middle East from a bomb attack. Strangely, a few times he's been injured and has the scars to show it.[6]

In the same way we have learned how to "stir up the gift within us" like prophecy and speaking in tongues, we are also going to know how to "stir up" teleporting, bi-location, shifting dimensions and the working of wonders. It is the natural progression of growing up to maturity as a Spirit-Being.

Like natural technology, what once seemed magical in the past will over time become common and normal. Technology is surging. Get ready for the corresponding spiritual surge!

Believe for miraculous transports!

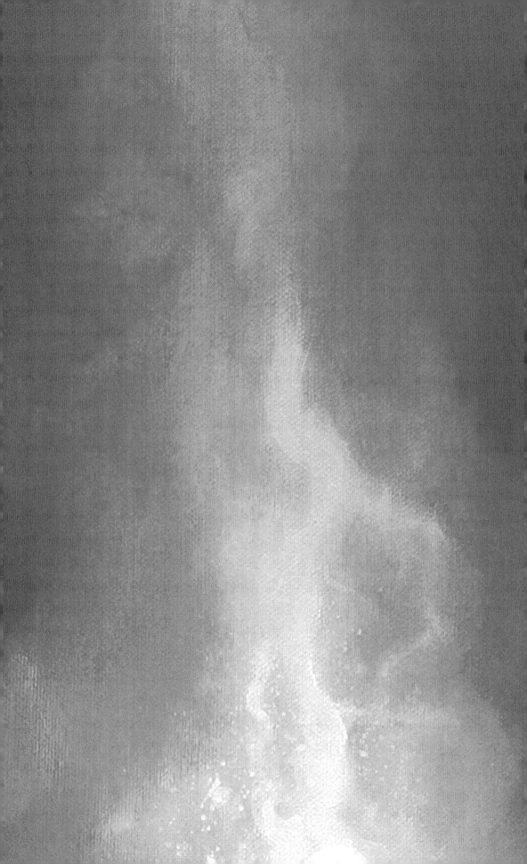

METAMORPHOSIS

As they watched, he (Jesus) began to change form (Mat 17:2, CJB).

I recently applied for a new passport. I had new up-to-date photos taken for it. I couldn't believe how much my face has changed in ten years. It's weird.

As you get older you realise the outside body is not really who you truly are. The body is an amazing gift and it serves a powerful purpose on Earth. It allows us to function in the seen world, yet it cannot ultimately define the deepest part of us.

In this chapter, I want to talk about a strange subject related to the body. I considered not putting it in the book as it is a little weird. But I felt before the Lord, it was right and I hope I've made the right call. Perhaps it will help someone reading this book understand some of their experiences. God cares about the one. This might be for you.

I want to talk about supernaturally changing appearance. Bible scholars call it "Metamorphosis" or "Transfiguration" which simply means:

A complete change of physical form or appearance (dictionary.com).

It seems in the "KAINOS" life, physical change is very possible. Most people know the transfiguration story on the mountain. It was an amazing moment of Jesus showing his closest friends who he really was in his Divine Nature. He suddenly changed form.

His appearance changed dramatically in their presence (Mat 17:2, AMP).

Sunlight poured from his face and his clothes became bright white as light. In that moment I believe they glimpsed the future of our species.

This was not the only time Jesus altered his physical form. This is something rarely discussed in Church life, yet it is clearly important enough to be mentioned in the scriptures. Just think about the following strange verses in the Gospels:

They were not able to recognize who he was (Luke 24:16).
She thought he was the man in charge of the garden (John 20:15).
The disciples did not know that it was Jesus (John 21:4).
Not one of the disciples dared to ask, "Who are You?" (John 21:12).

It is a mystery to me why Jesus changed appearance in the Gospels. I guess each time it showed a different attribute of his Divine Nature. Perhaps it taught his friends to see him through the Spirit not the flesh. To recognise him through cardio-gnosis which is the way Heaven works.

History records many times Jesus appeared in disguise to the saints. The famous monastic pioneer St. Martin of Tours[1] once shared his last cloak with a homeless beggar in the freezing cold. Martin later saw a vision of Jesus wearing the cloak in Heaven rejoicing with the saints and angels. Jesus had appeared to him in another form, the form of a humble beggar. Amazing!

One of my friends, Lorna, from Scotland, had a similar honour. She met Jesus in the supermarket cafe on her 50th birthday. Jesus looked like an ordinary man. He started a conversation with Lorna and they ate fish together. They talked for some time and His words were captivating. It was only after the lunch Lorna realised it was really Jesus. It was hidden from her at the time. What a happy birthday present! God has an amazing sense of humour! Wouldn't you like to see Jesus? I think you can (John 17:24).

Other times in Scripture, we read of even more astonishing and mystical forms of transformation happening to Jesus. Here John saw him with white hair and eyes of fire:

And having turned I saw... One like the Son of Man, clothed with a garment down to the feet and girded about the chest with a golden band. His head and hair *were* white like wool, as white as snow, and His eyes like a flame of fire (Rev 1:12-14).

As if that wasn't crazy enough for one experience, beloved John later saw Jesus, like a lamb with seven eyes and seven horns. Truly bizarre and fearful.

And I looked, and behold, in the midst of the throne and of the four living creatures, and in the midst of the elders, stood a Lamb as though it had been slain, having seven horns and seven eyes, which are the seven Spirits of God sent out into all the earth (Rev 5:6).

As we behold him, we become like him. Is it possible to engage so deeply with the Lord that you briefly take on his appearance? It's hard to imagine but entirely possible according to the Bible:

Now all of us, with our faces unveiled, reflect the glory of the Lord as if we are mirrors; and so we are being transformed, metamorphosed, into His same image from one radiance of glory to another, just as the Spirit of the Lord accomplishes it (2 Cor 3:18, VOI).

Perhaps this is what happened to Moses after seeing the Lord face to face. We read in some older translations that his face wasn't just shining, but that he also had something like horns.

And when Moses came down from the mount Sinai, he held the two tables of the testimony, and he knew not that his face was horned from the conversation of the Lord (Ex 34:29, DRB).

This comes from the word "*qaran*" which means "to send out rays or to display or grow horns, be horned". Some old paintings even show Moses with these unusual horns.

I'm not being dogmatic about any of this. It's just really interesting and makes you think about what is possible. The Bible is much weirder than we think. Bill Johnson laughs when pastors say "I just want what's in the Bible." He's like "Are you sure!?" the Bible is pretty crazy!

Looking at the lives of the saints, there are hundreds of metamorphosis stories frequently involving their faces shining or looking angelic. In this next story, Catholic saint Bernardino Realino transfigured in ecstasy:

An extraordinary radiance transformed his countenance. Some declared that they had seen sparks coming from all over his body like sparks of fire, while others declared that the glow coming from his countenance dazzled them on more than one occasion, so that they could no longer distinguish his features and had to turn away their gaze for fear of straining their eyes.[2]

Occasionally you do find a metamorphosis story that stretches the box even further. This is one of my favourites. It comes from the life of Patrick in Ireland. It's inspiring!

It is told that Saint Patrick and his men were travelling to the king's court, when he discovered that the Druids (Celtic priests) had prepared an ambush for him. As they walked, the saint and his followers chanted the sacred Lorica, or Deer's Cry, that later became known as the St. Patrick's Breastplate Prayer, claimed, again with some uncertainty, to have been created by the saint. According to the myth the Druids did not see the saint and his followers pass, but saw only a gentle doe followed by twenty fawns.[3]

I have actually seen a person change appearance. Not as dramatically as Patrick, but I once saw a young prophet change right in front of me. I saw his face shift. It looked like the physical face of Jesus. His hair grew longer, the shape of his nose and eyes changed, he grew a short beard. It was astonishing!

Before I could fully grasp what was happening, his original face snapped back into place. The form of Jesus was gone instantly. I was so astonished I told no-one at the time, not even this young prophet. It amazed me.

Truly a wonder!

Since then I have come across similar phenomena a number of times. It has even happened to me. Once whilst ministering in Wales, my face changed during the teaching session to the amazement of some visitors. They said I looked like another person. My mum saw this and said it didn't look like me. She found it hard to describe but knew it was the Lord. I was not aware this was taking place. I was deeply absorbed in God.

Maybe this is also what happened to Stephen in the book of Acts:

Everyone sitting in the *Sanhedrin* stared at Stephen and saw that his face looked like the face of an angel (Acts 6:15, CJB).

Somehow Stephen's face looked different. Some translations say they "gazed intently" (AMPC) at him, captivated by his appearance. It is an unusual scripture.

As with all good things, there is a counterfeit from satan. He likes to steal and twist and abuse the spiritual world for his own selfish ends. My good friend in ministry, Grant Mahoney, witnessed first hand a witch doctor change shape. This story is recorded on one of our Podcasts called "Sonship" (available free online):

We were on a missions trip and we heard laughing outside the tent. I opened the tent and saw a hyena outside. I almost wet my pants! There were five or four of us in the tent and we all saw the hyena. We rebuked it and as we all rebuked it we saw it change into a witch doctor and run away. This stuff is real![4]

They may be able to do some spiritual wonders like the Egyptian sorcerers (see Exodus 7:8-11), yet there is coming a time when the sons will exceed their abilities in every respect. They will be forced to admit:

This is the [supernatural] finger of God (Ex 8:19, AMP).

Forerunner Grant Mahoney is one that is beginning to do this already.

Before you read this next story, I want you to know, Grant is a man of integrity who walks intimately with the Father. He is all about Jesus. He is someone I trust. I believe his account.

There are things we are going to do that will mind-freak people... In my own life this has happened to me six times. For the same reason - where women were about to be raped. I was there (in the Spirit) and I transformed into a bear, and dealt with the rapists. And it has happened two other times when I was in a situation where my life was in threat. I transformed into a bear again and the threat left. Do I have a grid for that? No. It just happened. I don't have an explanation for it.

Amazing! That is justice. Rescuing. Saving. Delivering. Sounds like Heaven to me!

Grant is not the only one to have shape-altering experiences. I have met others having similar manifestations on my travels. They have asked to stay hidden, preferring to be unknown, their stories remaining secret. I honour that.

I realise how stretching all this is. The Bible itself testifies there are new things to come that "no eye has seen, nor ear heard" (1 Cor 2:9). We must adjust to the Dove as he ventures off the familiar paths into new territory. Remember, "with God ALL THINGS are possible" (Mat 19:26).

In prophetic experiences, I have been shown some of the future changes. I have seen that some missionaries will be teleported to Muslim nations in an instant, appearing to crowds as the same ethnicity and speaking the local language. Once more there will be convincing proofs of the resurrection that bring many sons to glory.

In a trance-vision, the Lord showed me a majestic Light Being. Shaped like a person, it was sparkling with coloured energy. It looked like living sparkles of amber, with the grace of music. Ribbons of light and colour. I knew when I saw it, that there was nothing else like it. It was unique. I was in a state of awe looking at it. Stunned.

The Lord said "Do you know what this is?" I did not. He said "It is the beauty of the human spirit." He paused to allow me to digest this. Then he said this heavyweight line, "The human spirit has a limitless capacity to grow."

The implications penetrated my heart. I saw by revelation we will keep growing and growing, even beyond angels and created things. That we are the crown jewel of the cosmos. His Bride. Like nothing else.

I asked the Lord to give me a scripture to support this. Even though it was very powerful I like to also see it in the Word. I have found Papa is happy to give me scriptures. He said "That's easy; 1 John 3:2!" which (paraphrased) reads:

But now we are sons of God... but what we will be - we don't know!

Wow! Now we are sons, but what we will be, we do not yet know. Think about that. None of us know what truly awaits us. Our future is glorious. I love that!

Read it again in the Message:

But friends, that's exactly who we are: children of God. And that's only the beginning. Who knows how we'll end up! What we know is that when Christ is openly revealed, we'll see him - and in seeing him, become like him. All of us who look forward to his coming stay ready, with the glistening purity of Jesus' life as a model for our own.

All we know is that our present body is just a seed. The tree will be far greater.

There are also celestial bodies and terrestrial bodies; but the glory of the celestial is one, and the glory of the terrestrial is another. There is one glory of the sun, another glory of the moon, and another glory of the stars; for one star differs from another star in glory...

The first man was of the earth, made of dust; the second Man is the Lord from heaven. As was the man of dust, so also are those

who are made of dust; and as is the heavenly Man, so also are those who are heavenly. And as we have borne the image of the man of dust, we shall also bear the image of the heavenly Man (1 Cor 15:40-49).

It's too much to handle! It's no wonder we get intoxicated with joy! The Gospel just gets bigger and bigger the more you drink it!

We stand fully identified in the new creation renewed in knowledge according to the pattern of the EXACT IMAGE of our Creator (Col 3:10, MIR).

Our bodies can't define us any longer.

DIMENSIONAL SHIFTS

"God wants us to understand and to believe that we are more truly in heaven than on earth." (Julian of Norwich)[1]

By God's design, every human limitation we have imagined is going to be broken through new spiritual pioneers. Like the industrial revolution before, we are in a spiritual technology revolution that will ultimately take the Earth forward into a glorious age of peace and advancement.

One of the limitations to be broken is our physical bodies being captive to the seen dimensional plane. Up until now it has been normal for our bodies to stay here whilst our spirits have moved into the Heavens or across the Earth. This is going to change.

From the very beginning we were made to be multidimensional. Like 'Jacob's Ladder' we are Gates and Doors (plural) to multiple planes of dimensional existence:

Mighty gates: lift up your heads! Ancient doors: rise up high! (Psalms 24:7, CEB).

Enoch is a key role model for now. He was the seventh from Adam. Seven is the number of the end, the fulfilment, rest, the Divine. Enoch hosted his body in the Spirit. He was taken into Heaven for long periods of time. Eventually disappearing from the seen. He phased through many dimensions by faith.

BY FAITH Enoch was taken away (NKJV) ...caught up (AMP) ... translated (DAR) ...removed (DLNT) ...translated (KJV) (Heb 11:5).

Eventually, Enoch skipped death and now lives as an "Everliving One". Ancient yet as fresh as a youth. Transformed in body, soul and spirit. Transcendent.

He shows us some of what it means to live "Beyond Human" - immortal, ever young, transdimensional and full of the Spirit. Enoch shows it is possible to transcend death.

Up until now, the Church has mostly been contained and confined by this lower dimension. Captive to the seen. Our bodies have remained limited. This is going to change!

Let's explore this. How far can we go?

Looking again at the one perfect Blueprint, Jesus Christ, we see some really interesting things. Jesus moved dimensions both in the spirit and in the body. He was able to pull his body out of the visible world into the unseen as required.

In the following story from the Gospel of John, we read about an angry religious crowd who wanted to kill Jesus. The crowd was so angry they picked up stones to kill Jesus inside the temple. There was nowhere to hide! Nowhere to run! Jesus was trapped. Surrounded! How did he get out of this?

They took up stones to throw at Him; but Jesus HID Himself (John 8:59).

They picked up stones to hurl at him, but Jesus DISAPPEARED (PHI).

He escaped the angry mob by vanishing. He shifted dimensions. Like angels he was still on the Earth but not in the same world! I bet it happened so quickly the people couldn't process it in their minds. They were stunned!

Not only did Jesus disappear, but in this unusual state he was able to pass right through solid objects, strangely even right through people.

Going through the midst of them, and so passed by (YLT).

This is the unstoppable force of living from the 'Books of Heaven' (see Psalms 139:16). It wasn't His time to die. He could not be stopped until the cross. He lived in convergence with Heaven. A higher truth than visible light.

This wasn't the only time Jesus did this. Jesus made the religious crowd so crazy with his teaching! He didn't say what they wanted to hear and challenged them to the core. He made them mad ('full of wrath'). One time they grabbed him and threw him out of the city. Look at what happened next:

They rose up and thrust Him out of the city; and they led Him to the brow of the hill on which their city was built, that they might throw Him down over the cliff (Luke 4:28-30).

You can't gently walk through a crowd of blood-thirsty religionists. They were hyped up and ready to kill. It must have been a very dramatic moment. Did his disciples think it was all over for Jesus? Was this the end?

Imagine their shock when Jesus shifted dimensions again! Was he invisible or partly invisible? Did he look like a ghost? All we know is he walked THROUGH them.

Then passing through the midst of them, He went His way (Luke 4:30).

That sounds so nice... passing through them. Jesus probably scared the life out of them!

(Why don't they ever show this in Hollywood Jesus movies?)

Another time, Jesus not only shifted realms, he phased so much he looked ethereal like a ghost and became anti-gravimetric! Even gravity became a lesser truth.

When the disciples saw Jesus walking on the water, they thought

he was a ghost, and they started screaming. All of them saw him and were terrified. But at that same time he said, "Don't worry! I am Jesus. Don't be afraid." (Mark 6:49, CEV).

He looked like a ghost - transparent, not really here, transdimensional!

As we drink deeper and deeper of the union we have with the Divine Essence, beautiful-amazing things will happen to the body. The frequency of our bodies will shift and we will find we are not "really from here", we are "not of this world."

I call it being "Hidden here and revealed there".

As the English mystic Julian of Norwich said "We are more in Heaven than on Earth."[1]

Disappearing is moving our body into another dimensional world. It is where the angels walk. Where the 'Cloud of Witnesses' are seen. It surrounds us. It envelops everything.

It may surprise you but some saints KNEW how to PHASE SHIFT like this at will. They understood the spiritual technology behind it. One such saint who disappeared was Francis of Paola. He was known through his lifetime as a great miracle worker. In this story, Francis found himself mobbed by eager followers after visiting the governor. He was stuck in the swarming crowd.

When he was about to leave, people swarmed around the governors palace to see and be near him. Their great enthusiasm for the Saint was expressed by tearing off bits of his clothing - which the Saint surprisingly permitted.

God would renew his clothing as fast as it was being torn away. Spectators were amazed to see that after scores of people had torn away pieces from his hood and tunic, they were both still miraculously whole.

Finding it impossible to make his way through the crowd which was closely packed in the square, and being somewhat embarrassed by the adulation, the Saint suddenly disappeared before the people's eyes, much to their confusion. One moment he was there the next moment he was gone. His companions much to their amazement found him waiting for them outside the walls, ready to begin their journey.[2]

I love the humility of the saints, they were not seeking fame but living for God's glory.

Saint Gerard Majella is another well-loved Catholic saint. He lived a "KAINOS" life and manifested great power. Here's another story from Joan C. Cruz's inspiring book *Mysteries Marvels and Miracles in the lives of the Saints*, a book I highly recommend.

One day at the monastery at Caposele the Saint received permission to make a day's retreat of prayer and recollection in his room. A little later the Father Rector needed him and sent someone to fetch him. The Saint could not be found, although everyone in the house searched for him. Dr. Santorelli, the monastery's physician at one time exclaimed, "We have lost Brother-Gerard!"

Dr. Santorelli took one of the brothers with him for another search and went to the Saint's room, which measured ten feet square. The room contained only a poor bed and a little table, without any furniture which would prevent him being seen. He was nowhere to be found.

Finally, one of the religious realized that the Saint would surely come forward at the time of Holy communion, and so they waited.[3]

Ha! I love that. Communion is saint bait! Guaranteed to bring them out of hiding!

The story continues:

Exactly as predicted the Saint was seen at that particular moment. On being asked where he had been, the Saint answered, "In my room." When the religious told the Saint about the various places **they had searched for him, he made no reply. Then under obedience to tell what happened, the Saint explained "Fearing to be distracted in my retreat, I asked Jesus Christ for the grace to become invisible."**

Dr. Santorelli was still very curious and kept pressing St Gerard for answers.

Taking the doctor by the arm, the Saint guided him to his cell and pointed out the little stool where he had been sitting the whole time they were searching for him. Then the Saint whispered to the doctor, "...sometimes I make myself very little."

This miracle became so well known locally, the little children would say "Let us play Brother Gerard" and go and play hide-and-seek. Can you imagine this again today? I can. I am convinced it is coming. We are going to be astonished again.

In fact, in some places these wonders have already begun. Maybe you've read about Brother Yun from China? In his book *The Heavenly Man*, Yun shares an absolutely amazing story about how he escaped prison:

Somehow the Lord seemed to blind the guard. He was staring directly at me, yet his eyes didn't acknowledge my presence at all. I expected him to say something, but he just looked through me as if I was invisible. He didn't say a word. I continued past him and didn't look back. I knew I could be shot in the back at any moment... I continued walking down the stairs, but nobody stopped me and none of the guards said a word to me![4]

Amazingly in broad day light he walked past several guards right out of the front gate. No one had ever escaped that high security prison before. It was a miracle!

This dimensional shifting is not limited to the persecuted Chinese church. It is also happening in the western world. In his book *Supernatural Transportation*, Michael Van Vlymen shares an incredible moment, where he walked through a crowd of people. Michael writes:

I was seeking the Lord one evening when I suddenly found myself at an outdoor concert venue not far from our house. There were many young people there at this concert who were very obviously drunk or stoned or both. I saw crowds of people walking in my direction and I felt I was supposed to walk in the other direction so I did. At first I was trying to move and turn sideways to navigate my way through the crowd, but I realised that I was in fact walking through people. As I realised this, I didn't even try to avoid them. I just walked right through them. I could tell that many people were visibly upset at experiencing this and I would guess that they probably thought it was due to the alcohol or drugs.[5]

Why would God initiate such a bizarre act? Michael believes it was to smash people out of their addictions. It was actually a powerful manifestation of grace to awaken slumbering hearts. I believe it!

I believe this type of sign and wonder is going to increase. We are coming into days of shock and awe. The joy and fear of God is coming upon us again, as Hosea prophesied:

They shall fear the Lord and His goodness in the latter days (Hos 3:5, NKJV).

In fact, it is already happening. Forerunner Nancy Coen was once sent by the Spirit into a satanic night club. It was one of the darkest places you can imagine, full of demonic people. Everyone turned to look at Nancy. Standing there before the crowd, she began to cry and groan in deep intercession for the people. Nancy felt the longing of creation echoing throughout her being (see Romans 8:22). All Nancy did was cry. She walked out of the club thinking she had failed.

Two years later Nancy met the (former) high priestess from the night club. She told Nancy what really happened. As Nancy cried, she vanished into thin air and re-appeared as a brilliant blinding light in front of the satanists. The supernatural light struck the high priestess completely blind.

Her friends panicked and wanted to take her to the ER. However, she knew it was Jesus. She was taken home instead and there God healed her and delivered her. Over the next two years, this one transformed woman led most of the the satanists at that club to Jesus. She is now moving in powerful prophetic ministry. Amazing![6]

This era is not going to be simply business as usual.

**The First Adam received life,
the Last Adam is a life-giving Spirit
(1 Cor 15:45, MSG).**

The implications of the Gospel are massive.
Death will be swallowed up by Life.

INEDIA:
PROLONGEDFASTING

His disciples urged Him, saying, "Rabbi, eat." But He said to them, "I have food to eat of which you do not know." Therefore the disciples said to one another, "Has anyone brought Him anything to eat?" (John 4:31-33).

Are you beginning to see a glimpse of the wonder of the Gospel yet? It's amazing. We will never stop enjoying it. Never stop exploring it. Angels are in awe of it!

The more I have experienced mystic prayer and engaged heavenly realms, the more I've had to re-examine many assumptions about the body, the mind, the spirit, distance, dimensions, intellect and more.

In the Co-Life something amazingly indescribable has happened to each one of us. We're only just beginning to realise the implications of the Gospel. We have been fully re-defined in Christ. Chew on this:

The terms, co-crucified and co-alive define me now. Christ in me and I in Him (Gal 2:20, MIR)!

Human definitions don't fit us anymore. Who we were before is finished and gone. It was co-crucified and died. The new Co-Alive has arrived! In light of the Gospel, let's allow God to unravel the past thinking and renew our minds. The way we think changes the world we see. There are more possibilities to explore.

Let's look at another challenging shift for us. I want to challenge the dependancy on earthly sources of nourishment - that is food and water.

Let's re-examine again what it means to live "Beyond Human" limitations, beginning with Jesus and the woman at the well. We talked about this in the chapter on "Infused Knowledge". This time I want to focus on a different angle of the story. As you well know, in this story Jesus spent time restoring a broken woman. She was astonished and ran to tell the town.

And at this point His disciples came, and they marvelled that He talked with a woman; yet no one said, "What do You seek?" or, "Why are You talking with her?"

The woman then left her water pot, went her way into the city, and said to the men, "Come, see a Man who told me all things that I ever did. Could this be the Christ?" Then they went out of the city and came to Him.

In the meantime His disciples urged Him, saying, "Rabbi, eat." But He said to them, "I have food to eat of which you do not know." (John 4:27-32).

Jesus went from being "wearied from the journey" to suddenly having a supernatural Divine energy. The disciples knew Jesus well and could see he was refreshed. They asked "Did someone give him some food?" They were bemused (John 4:1-42).

We know Jesus loved to feast and was happier than anyone else (Heb 1:9). He could eat and drink, and really loved the table times. He was accused of being a wine bibber (meaning a 'steady drinker') by the religious (Luke 7:34). Yet, eating it seems was for joy, not essential for life. Jesus could live without it:

I have food to eat of which you do not know.

There is a mystical secret here. Don't miss it.

In that moment of sitting at the well, obeying the Father, Jesus was infused with the Life of the Spirit. He said:

My food is to do the will of Him who sent Me, and to finish His work (John 4:34).

Jesus was full and satisfied in obeying the will of the Father! Replenished by joy!

This possibility exists for us also. We can live beyond dependance upon food. I know it's shocking, but keep reading. Let me explain it.

This "KAINOS" possibility of inedia is not about loss. No! It's about FEASTING from another Realm. We are eating and drinking from a Hidden Reality. We have accessed the Tree of Life (Revelation 2:7)! We are FAT and HAPPY on the fatness of the Lamb!

Christ, God's lamb, has been slain for us.
So let us FEAST UPON HIM (1 Cor 5:7-8, TLB).

For indeed Christ, our Passover, was sacrificed for us.
Therefore let us keep the FEAST (1 Cor 5:7-8).

They shall be abundantly satisfied with the fatness of thy house (Psalms 36:8, DAR).

They relish and feast on the abundance (Psalms 36:8, AMPC).

I love the Butter-Fat Gospel of Jesus Christ! It's one of my favourite messages when I travel. The Gospel is a mystical FEAST not a fast. His body is real food.

And Jesus said to them, "I am the bread of life. He who comes to Me shall never hunger, and he who believes in Me shall never thirst... For My flesh is food indeed and My blood is drink indeed. He who eats My flesh and drinks My blood abides in Me, and I in him." (John 6:35-58).

As this generation realises (more than any other) the message of the finished works of Jesus Christ and the promise of mystical union contained in the Gospel, we will mature and begin to live from the full consequences of being co-included in Christ.

When we unite ourselves with him, the impossible becomes possible.

Like Moses on the mountain who stood in the black cloud of the presence for weeks, we will find the presence sustains our bodies more than anything the visible world can offer.

So Moses went into the midst of the cloud and went up into the mountain. And Moses was on the mountain forty days and forty nights (Ex 24:18).

There is energy in union with our Creator. In him, we can access LIMITLESS LIFE.

I have experienced small glimpses of this. Sudden surges of supernatural energy that have lasted for days. I have woken up full of Life and had to run and run to burn it off. Often in preaching, the energy compels me to pace up and down and sometimes run around the room, letting out happy shouts to try and release some of the inner bliss. I have often been more energised at the end of the night than at the beginning.

In carefully taking the mystical elements of communion in the Spirit, I find I become profoundly conscious of God. I have felt a fullness, an inner wellbeing, that is hard to put into words. It is like an expansive sensation of being filled with perfection. The perfection of Love.

At certain times all appetite for eating seems to dissolve and become meaningless. I have often turned down the invitation for a post-conference meal at night. I am learning to honour the sensation, rather than shake it off with programmed human behaviour.

I am hoping this Life flow will continue to grow in me until I can continue for weeks under Divine energy just like the saints. There is a price. You have to chose to live in Christ. Turning into His love. Living in the conscious awareness of His presence.

Many of the saints understood this. They found the "Mystic Secret of

God which is Christ" (Col 2:2, AMPC). In John Crowder's brilliant book *The Ecstasy of Loving God*, John writes about this supernatural Inedia in Church history:

Medically it is impossible to go without water more than four days, without experiencing dehydration and death. But the mystics of the church, especially those who experienced intense ecstasy, have undergone inedia that would be impossible to believe if it were not so well documented. Alexandria Maria da Costa went from March 27, 1942, until her death on October 13, 1955, with only communion as her food each day. That is more than 13 years! The German mystic and stigmatist Therese Neumann (1898-1962) is perhaps the most amazing modern example. She went 40 years without food and more than 35 years without water, except for communion. Both she and Alexandria experienced no ill effects from this fasting, nor did their bodies eliminate waste.[1]

I have read many accounts of the Desert Fathers and the Celtic saints who lived alone on small islands, or wilderness places, existing on the minimum diet possible, sometimes just eating one small meal a day, without suffering harm.

In the following story St. Brendan and his friends were led to journey by the Lord to a small island. There they found a very old man who was sustained by God.

When Brendan came to the summit of the island, he saw two caves with a waterfall in front of them. As he stood before the caves, a very old man came toward him. "It is good for brethren to come together," he said and bade Brendan call the other men from the boat.

When they came, the old man greeted them and kissed them and called them by their own names one by one. Brendan was so amazed at the man's countenance, which was glorious, and by his knowing their names, that he wept and sobbed, saying, "I am not worthy to wear the monk's habit."

Brendan asked Paul (the hermit) how he came to that island and where he was from previously. Paul answered, "I was brought up in the monastery of Patrick for fifty years. I was in charge of the cemetery of the brothers. My Abbot one day pointed to the sea and said, 'Tomorrow go there and you will find a boat which will bear you to a place where you will remain until the day of your death.'

"I did as he told me and for three days I rowed and then left off the oars and I let the boat drift for seven days and let it be led by the Lord. Thus I came to this island and here I have stayed, giving myself to prayer and intercession." Paul continued, "The first day an otter came and brought me a fish to eat. After that the otter came every third day and brought the same. The stream and waterfall brought water, and I have been here to 90 years, and fifty with Patrick. Now at 140 years I am still awaiting the day of my account."[2]

Isn't that amazing?! I am challenged whenever I read these stories. These people lived 100% for God, immersing themselves in Him. Living in union with Heaven & Earth.

I think it's time for us to change! I want to be FREE!

In the 1980s, Brother Yun (lovingly called "The Heavenly Man") was imprisoned and beaten nearly to death. In squalid conditions he fasted water and food for 74 days. The whole prison and security services knew of this incredible miracle.[3]

When his mother and wife were finally allowed to see him, Yun said to them he was hungry. They thought he meant for food. But he said he was hungry and thirsty for souls. This is the thirst Jesus felt at the cross. The longing for humanity to be reconciled.

The Blueprint is Christ. As the Resurrected One, does Jesus really need to be sustained by Earth food any longer? We know Jesus is able to eat it and enjoy it. Scripture shows he ate with the disciples after the resurrection:

But while they still did not believe for joy, and marvelled, He said to them, "Have you any food here?" So they gave Him a piece of a broiled fish and some honeycomb. And He took it and ate in their presence (Luke 24:41-43).

Food is good. We are free to eat it and enjoy it, but we must not be limited by it.

There is a higher way emerging. As the Lord wills, as God permits, a generation will transcend human limitations, even the old need for food and sleep. We will manifest a hidden higher Divine Life that sustains the lower visible life.

You prepare a table before me in the presence of my enemies (Psalms 23:5).

To him who overcomes I will give to eat from the tree of life, which is in the midst of the Paradise of God (Rev 2:7).

I will give of the fountain of the water of life freely to him who thirsts (Rev 21:6).

This is the "KAINOS" way of living and thinking, believing that even now we can 'taste of the power of the age to come' (Hebrews 6:5). We can manifest the future here and now.

We may not have the full package showing up yet, but don't you want to find out how much we can see now?! How far we can go? I know I want to see change in me.

I am prophesying to you, to those who read this book with child-like hearts.

He leads me beside the still waters.
He restores my soul; (Psalms 23:1-3)

To a generation who have fallen in love with the Shepherd, we will find the Source of Life. Eventually, there will be a company of people that live forever.

As the living Father sent Me, and I live because of the Father, so he who feeds on Me will live because of Me. This is the bread which came down from heaven - not as your fathers ate the manna, and are dead. He who eats this bread will live forever (John 6:57).

Inedia cannot be accomplished through human formulas, natural fasting or our inner strength of will. No! Please don't do that! As Jesus said:

I can of Myself do nothing (John 5:30).

Living in mystical union, the saints found the sustaining flow of Life:

For with You is the fountain of life (Psalms 36:9).

and again,

But whoever drinks of the water that I shall give him will never thirst. But the water that I shall give him will become in him a fountain of water springing up into everlasting life (John 4:14).

Saint Catherine of Sienna[4] was so full of God, she found it nearly impossible to eat! In fact eating food would make her sick. She lost her appetite entirely and lived off a small serving of daily communion.

I believe passionately, a company is emerging who will live this message out. Not from old human efforts but because they are drawn into "KAINOS" life beyond the veil. We may well eat, but we will not be sustained in the same way. We will break the hold.

Even more, some will be so full of life, they will live beyond the reach of death.

But now [that extraordinary purpose and grace] has been fully disclosed and realized by us through the appearing of our Saviour Christ Jesus who [through His incarnation and earthly ministry] abolished death [making it null and void] and brought life and immortality to light through the gospel (2 Tim 1:10, AMP).

Like Enoch, they will discover the power of an endless life.[5]

It was faith that kept Enoch from dying (Heb 11:5, GNT).

In the "KAINOS" era, death has lost its sting!

Get ready to see vastly extended life-spans, regeneration of youthfulness and immortality. This may seem hard to imagine now, but it is coming and sooner than you imagine.

In fact, it has already begun.

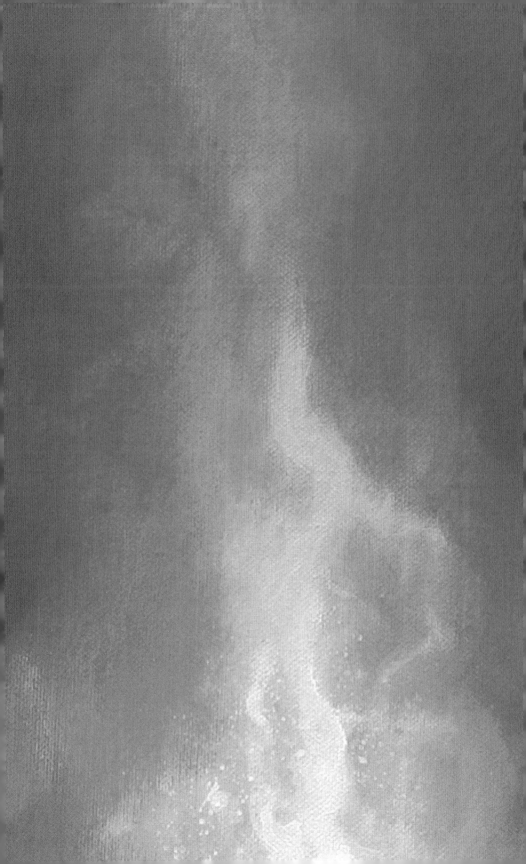

BEYONDSLEEP: REDEEMING THE NIGHT

"If you stand in the presence of the Father you don't need sleep."
Paul Keith Davis[1]

Did you know the average person sleeps eight hours a night? If you live to be 75, then you will have slept around 25 years. Can you believe that? 25 years of shut eye!

I don't know about you but I want my time here to count, even the night. I don't want to just zone out and wake up in the morning wondering what happened. That's not right!

I want to be in the Spirit in my sleep, conscious and aware, engaging the Kingdom Realm of the Father. I don't want to be unconscious and disconnected any longer. That seems less than what Scripture promises us. Just think about this:

But his delight is in the law of the Lord
And in His law he meditates day and night (Psalms 1:2).

How is it possible to meditate day and night? Again look at this clue:

I went to sleep, but my heart stayed awake (Song of Sol 5:2, AMPC).

So you can stay awake and be asleep?! Sounds amazing. I want it!

This is where we introduce another happy truth! The Gospel doesn't just change the day and fill it with new possibilities. It also changes the night into rich times of engaging Heaven and travelling in the Spirit. Entire nights immersed in the bliss of mystic union and having adventures in the nations and even the stars.

I have begun to experience some of it. I've had nights where I have been intentional in my focus on ascending into God. I have noticed that when I focus on Oneness, and being in Him, somehow more of Heaven opens up. It's the law of desire and focus.

Delight yourself also in the Lord, and He shall give you the desires of your heart (Psalms 37:4).

My friend Ian Clayton has learned it is both possible to live with little sleep and also remain conscious whilst sleeping, by hosting his body in his Spirit man. Ian used to get up earlier and earlier to pray. He was so hungry. Yet he always felt he didn't have enough time with the Father. He realised there was only so much he could physically do.

Eventually he found a solution. He learned to engage the Spirit and ascend during the night into the Mountain of God. Now he has some of his most profound experiences during sleep. When we minister together I always ask him "What happened last night?" He always has something new to share. Often something vital for the meetings.

He also lives for weeks with very little sleep at all, beyond natural limitations. I have seen him minister a full-on conference straight from the airport. That's an amazing feat when you've travelled from New Zealand and haven't slept once. That is "KAINOS" life.

Sound too good to be true? Then read on!

Let's gaze again at Jesus, the One that gives us a hope of greater things to come!

Now it came to pass in those days that He (Jesus) went out to the mountain to pray, and continued ALL NIGHT in prayer to God (Luke 6:12).

It seems for Jesus sleep was optional! Sometimes He was up all night in prayer.

What's more amazing about this is when you consider the hectic lifestyle Jesus had. He walked everywhere. Mentored a bunch of intense disciples. Healed the sick. Preached to multitudes. Dealt with the religious, and much more besides.

Yet He seemingly surpassed the natural laws and tapped into a higher dimensional reality. A reality that transcends normal sleep patterns. A lifestyle immersed in Life.

How is this possible? Can we do this also?

Prophet Paul Keith Davis was shown part of the answer. He had a profound visionary experience where he was shown Jesus praying on the mountain. Instead of trying to stay awake like Paul Keith expected, he saw Jesus was energised in the bliss of the Presence. He was not fighting off sleep nor counting the hours. He was caught up with Papa and the night seemed timeless. Jesus had to pull Himself away in the morning. The whole night was spent in rapture. Jesus rose refreshed at dawn, full of joy.

The Presence is the key to the mystery. Engaging the Presence of God is what opens the gateways of limitless possibilities. When we live in Him, all things are possible.

"If you stand in the presence of the Father you don't need sleep."
Paul Keith Davis[1]

I feel the night is so often wasted. I don't want to live like that anymore.

I know a growing number of people that are redeeming the night. They are breaking the human limitations of normal human patterns. People like Nancy Coen. She is challenging our understanding of what it means to live on Earth as it is in Heaven.

Listen to Nancy Coen's own testimony:

In all of the times I have been travelling in all of the nations, I have never, ever had jet-lag. Now when you travel millions of miles to say you have never ever had jet-lag is totally amazing. In fact on my trip over here (to New Zealand), the time it took me from when I left my house to get to their house, was 64 hours. And in that 64 hours I got one hour sleep. But when I got off the plane I was so excited to see everybody, so full of energy it didn't bother me that I hadn't had any sleep.

I've been in places in the caves of China where I actually preached five solid days without sitting down. Without taking a break, without ever taking a nap, or stopping for dinner or having a glass of water, without (going to) the bathroom.

How is that even possible? It's *not humanly possible*.

The way that it has become possible: I have begun to get the breakthrough to set my spirit in control of my soul and my body.[2]

Earlier in the year, when I started writing this book, I really hit a wall. I was thinking about all the things God has shown us about living "Beyond Human" and I realised how crazy it might sound to some people. I was considering giving up on the book.

Then a friend passed me Nancy Coen's teachings. I was astonished when I heard her echo the exact same ideas. I was so thrilled I listened to ten hours of Nancy straight. It was like honey to me. I couldn't get enough. She confirmed what I had seen. Not only that, but Nancy is actually living it out. Recently, I was with Nancy and she didn't sleep for the entire three days and looked full of energy. Amazing considering she is nearly 70!

If you've heard our Podcasts, you'll know we are really inspired by the lives of the Celtic saints. This company of simple believers walked in true apostolic authority and shaped the destiny of Ireland, Britain and beyond. They walked in power, love and profound humility. Like Nancy

Coen, they also often transcended the need for natural sleep.

Great demands were made of Cuthbert and between leading prayers and intensive periods of teaching he would go for short walks to refresh himself. Amid all the activity, though he worshipped with the community, he often sought time for quiet prayer, and on these occasions he would descend the cliffs to be near the sea.

One night, one of the brothers decided to follow him secretly, curious to see what Cuthbert was doing all night. With the spy following him, Cuthbert descended to the sea and entered the water until it came up to his neck. There in the water, with arms outstretched, he spent the night giving praise to God and singing to the sound of the waves. At day break, he went on the shore and began to pray again, kneeling on the sand.[3]

I have stood in the water near where this happened. It is even more astonishing when you consider how cold the sea water actually is around the UK. Ice cold! Incredible!

Francis of Assisi was another saint who lived "Beyond Human." As a radical young man, he stripped naked in protest and walked out on his great family wealth to touch the most lost and poorest of the poor. Initially he was homeless and mocked. A kind man called Bernard took pity on St. Francis and took him off the street into his home.

And so he invited him to supper in the evening and to lodge in his house, and St. Francis accepted and supped with him and lodged. Then Bernard had a bed prepared in his own chamber, where at night a lamp was always kept burning. And St. Francis, to conceal his sanctity, having entered into the chamber, forthwith cast himself upon the bed and feigned sleep. In like manner, Bernard, after a little while, laid himself down and began to snore loudly as if he were fast asleep. Presently, believing that Bernard was really asleep, St. Francis rose from his bed and began to pray, lifting his eyes and hands to heaven, and saying with great devotion and fervour, "My God, my God." And so saying and weeping continually, he remained until

morning, always repeating: "My God, my God," and nothing else.[4]

Witnessing this humble supernatural sleepless night had a massive impact on Bernard. From that day he was changed and became the first Franciscan monk. He went on to be a close friend to St. Francis, to care for the poor, to plant monasteries and to live a deeply mystical lifestyle. Often being caught up for days in ecstatic love trances, whilst walking in the forest. Pure bliss!

One of my other favourite saints is Catherine of Siena (truthfully I have so many saints I enjoy, they are like friends to me). She lived a consecrated life from a young age, beginning to see heavenly visions of Jesus at five or six. She was captivated by Love, to the point that:

(She) hardly slept for half-an-hour every two days. Yet she was never weary, or harassed, or fatigued.[5]

She was love sick. Love makes you forget to eat. Forget to sleep! Divine Love is Life!

Amazingly, some saints pushed this ability even further still. The Franciscan St. Colette went without any sleep for a whole year. Did you hear that?! A whole year. Imagine that! What would you do with the extra time? Imagine never being tired!

Even more amazingly, Agatha of the Cross, a Spanish Dominican did not sleep for the last eight years of her life. Incredible! I want that! I want to be in such closeness with God that even my body shares in the bliss.

But those who wait on the Lord shall renew their strength; they shall mount up with wings like eagles, they shall run and not be weary, they shall walk and not faint (Is 40:31).

Or as the VOICE translation says:

They will run - never winded, never weary. They will walk - never tired, never faint.

Prophet Paul Cain saw this verse would literally be fulfilled in the coming days. Paul saw in stunning clarity visions of the harvest. In these movie-like experiences, Paul saw with exceptional detail there would be stadium gatherings in cities all over the world. In these powerful revival meetings, unknown people were preaching the mysteries for days without stop. They would not rest or sit for days at a time, and yet showed no signs of fatigue or tiredness.

This is coming! I believe it and live to see it happen. This is why I am writing. I believe we have to press on and challenge the limitations. We must begin to grow in our capacity to imagine a bigger life. A wild crazy life that transforms the world!

Nancy Coen, Ian Clayton and the historic saints show it is possible. More than that, Jesus demonstrated it and invited us to do the same. If it is possible then I want it!

I dare you to believe it. Tonight as you go to bed, engage Heaven. Keep practising. Eventually something new will happen. Small keys open up big doors. Amen!

---

*Expanded Discussion: Did Jesus sleep?

I want to propose something to you that the Father taught me by revelation. You are free to think differently if it doesn't resonate. We are all powerful to think.

Holy Spirit asked me **"Do you think Jesus was sleeping in the boat?"** (see Luke 8:23).

I wondered at that. I thought about the storm, the water lashing in, the waves, the loud panic of the disciples. It doesn't exactly sound like a dreamy moment. More like a cold soaking mess! Who would sleep in that?

Holy Spirit responded: "He was caught up to the Father in spiritual ecstasy."

I was amazed! That made so much sense to me.

I've spent several years studying mystical theology, ecstasies and trances, reading the lives of the saints. I knew that in the higher states of mystic prayer, the person becomes unaware of the physical body. They are detached from "the sensible facilities" and completely swallowed up by Divine Love. In this state the saint can even seem to be almost dead and in extreme cases, stop breathing entirely.

I researched the word used by Luke for Jesus being "asleep." He chose an unusual word in his Gospel. It is only used here once in the entire New Testament. The word he chose was "aphypnoō" (Strongs G879).[6]

It comes from two other root words. The first is "apo" which means: "the separation of a part from the whole". The second root word "hypnos" is where we get the word "hypnotised" from, which is a sleep-like state. It also means "spiritual torpor" which is "a state of suspended physical powers and activities".

Amazing! This is almost an exact fit for the descriptions we read in Catholic theology for mystical ecstatic states. I want to propose this is what happened to Jesus in the boat. He was using the boat-time to be fully immersed in the Father. I am sure it happened often. Time out with Papa! A welcome recess from crowds.

I am not saying categorically Jesus didn't sleep, especially as a baby. What I am saying is that He transcended slavery to sleep (see Mat 26:40) as a mature Son. Sleep was not the master. He came from a Higher Place and even the night served Him.

But his delight is in the law of the Lord
And in His law he meditates day and night (Psalms 1:2).

Day and night! I love that!
Come on! Let's take back the night!

MASTERY OVER CREATION

The earth helped the woman, and the earth opened its mouth and swallowed up the flood (Rev 12:16, NKJV).

Our great grandparents Adam and Eve, had a powerful mandate towards creation. As the intimate friends of the Divine, they were commissioned to subdue the chaos of the Earth, and replenish (renew and fuel) the land back into the beauty and joy of Eden.

Be fruitful, and multiply, and replenish the earth, and subdue it: and have dominion (Gen 1:28, KJV).

What an awesome plan! Can you imagine Earth today if they had accomplished the task? I often imagine the Earth completely healed, and Adam's many ancestors moving outwards into the cosmos to shape other planets and stars back to life also. I imagine Mars restored and alive. It would have been incredible to be born into that era.

Sadly, we were born into a different world. The consequence of the tragic fall of man was a twisting of our relationship with the Planet and the living beings on it. The whole thing corrupted. It turned nasty! Thorns, toiling, animals killing animals.

This relationship with Earth was further damaged through Cain killing Abel. When Cain spilled blood, Earth withdrew its strength.

When you cultivate the ground, it shall no longer yield its strength [it will resist producing good crops] for you (Gen 4:12, AMP).

That's an astonishing verse! Earth is able to resist us or help us. This is another great mystery the Church has mostly overlooked. We have a dynamic relationship with Earth. It actually responds to us! In some way we don't understand it is alive.

Paul even implied that all created matter is somehow aware and waiting on us. Read this familiar passage again slowly. Try and take it in. It's incredible!

For all of creation is waiting, yearning for the time when the children of God will be revealed. You see, all of creation has collapsed into emptiness, not by its own choosing, but by God's. Still He placed within it a *deep and abiding* hope that creation would one day be liberated from its slavery to corruption and experience the glorious freedom of the children of God. For we know that all creation groans *in unison* with birthing pains up until now (Rom 8:19-22, VOI).

Creation has a "deep and abiding hope" for you to learn your relationship with it and to see it free. I realise we've barely begun to understand that.

Maybe, just maybe, we're now ready to learn. As "KAINOS" sons, perhaps it's time for us to realise we are made to join God's creative initiative and help nature.

Prophet Bob Jones used to say we are the "Shields of the Earth." That it is our job, our role to help protect the Earth from disaster.

For the shields of the earth belong to God (Psalms 47:9, NKJV). Earth's guardians belong to God (Psalms 47:9, CEB).

We should be intimately aware of the Earth and nature. It is in our mandate to protect it.

Prophet John Paul Jackson said:

There is a reason God did not simply speak us into existence, as He

did the vegetation, the animals, the moon and stars. Instead, He chose to create us out of the Earth. He shaped us with His fingers - from the soil. Why would He do that? Could it be that humans have a relationship with the Earth and the Earth has relationship with us that we don't yet understand? Could it be that just as it was with Cain, our choices affect the Earth?[1]

The Bible is crammed full of stories of the dynamic relationship we have with creation:

The ravens brought him (Elijah) bread and meat in the morning, and bread and meat in the evening; and he drank from the brook (1 Kings 17:6).

And they (the animals) went into the ark to Noah, two by two, of all flesh in which *is* the breath of life (Gen 7:15).

Moses lifted his hand and struck the rock twice with his rod; and water came out abundantly (Numb 20:11).

There are many other examples in scripture. It seems the Bible is full of what the Catholic theologians call "Nature Mystics!" It seems our destiny is tied with creation!

From the beginning of his ministry, Jesus showed us, we are supposed to be a convergence point for nature and Heaven. Look at this:

And He was there in the wilderness forty days, tempted by Satan, and was with the wild beasts; and the angels ministered to Him (Mark 1:13).

In a time of great personal trial "wild beasts" and "angels" gathered around him. Earth and Heaven respond to sonship.

This is the Pattern of our new species. We are supposed to bring harmony between realms. Merge seen and unseen. There is a magnetic force within us that draws creation and draws the angelic realm. It is the law of Life.

Jesus also revealed we are meant to manage the weather or as it says in Genesis "take dominion and subdue it."

Then He arose and rebuked the wind and the raging of the water. And they ceased, and there was a calm. But He said to them, "Where is your faith?" And they were afraid, and marvelled, saying to one another, "Who can this be? For He commands even the winds and water, and they obey Him!" (Luke 8:24-25).

If nature is out of balance it's our fault.

Why do I say this?

The clue is in the story above. Jesus rebuked them and asked them in essence why THEY had not done it. They had worked miracles. Where was their faith?

Sometimes calling out to God is a lower truth than us moving in Kingdom Reality. We are here to shield the Earth, and as we hold it in our heart in love, we can shape it.

I believe this is also true of most earthquakes and hurricanes, drought, heavy snowstorms and the like. The media call them "Acts of God", but I prefer to think of them as "Due to the inaction of Ecclesia." We are the government, the 'Earth Shields' after all.

Weather management is an important part of living in this era. We have been involved in shaping the weather many times, sometimes with astonishing results.

Once we were ministering in Brisbane Australia, and the sky was blue without a cloud in sight. They told us it hadn't rained for three months. I was amazed. I asked them why they hadn't changed that. They looked surprised at the idea of making it rain.

We prayed it would rain again, but not until we were on the plane home in three days time. We wanted to enjoy as much sunshine as possible!

Three days later on the way to the airport, we could see storm clouds filling the sky. It looked beautiful. We sat on the plane and as I looked out the window the rain began to fall on the glass. Just like we prayed! We laughed! Everything was perfect!

Other times, the Lord has asked us to change UK weather patterns at strategic moments. Once for a whole winter we kept back the snow storms. It was amazing. The weather office had predicted a terrible winter. The UK Newspapers couldn't work out what was going on. Instead of snow we had sunshine! In fact the number one sellers in January were salads and BBQs.[2] It was hilarious!

Yet Jesus didn't just manage storms. He moved in mastery over the wild life.

But Simon answered and said to Him, "Master, we have toiled all night and caught nothing; nevertheless at Your word I will let down the net." And when they had done this, they caught a great number of fish, and their net was breaking. So they signalled to *their* partners in the other boat to come and help them. And they came and filled both the boats, so that they began to sink (Luke 5:5-7).

Can you imagine fishing like that? Why not? For Jesus is the Pattern of us.

And again (a rather bizarre and wonderful) story:

Go to the sea, cast in a hook, and take the fish that comes up first. And when you have opened its mouth, you will find a piece of money (Mat 17:27).

Jesus could have created the coin in his hand. Why do it this way? Perhaps it was to demonstrate the partnership we have with creation? Whatever the case, I love it!

Nature miracles didn't stop with Jesus. The saints loved nature and nature loved them in return. Perhaps you've seen paintings of saints surrounded by animals?

The Franciscan monks were particularly engaged with the wild. They loved nature and God used that love many times to transform entire communities. In the following story, St. Anthony was preaching in a city called Rimini. They were a stubborn and difficult group of people. After many days of hard preaching they still wouldn't listen.

Therefore, one day, by Divine inspiration, St. Anthony went to the bank of the river. Standing on the shore between the sea and the river, he began to speak to the fishes, as though he was a preacher sent to them: "Hear the word of God, you fishes of the sea and of the river, since the infidel heretics refuse to hear it." When he had said this, there came to him on the river bank so vast a multitude of fishes... All of them held their heads out of the water and gazed attentively on the face of St. Anthony, remaining there in great peace and gentleness of order... The longer St. Anthony preached, the more did the multitude of fish increase... The people of the city began to run there to see the miracle this marvellous and clear, they were pricked in their hearts, and all cast themselves at the feet of St. Anthony to hear his words.[3]

Probably one of the groups of saints who understood this symbiotic relationship with nature the most, were the Celtic saints of Ireland and Britain. They saw themselves intrinsically entwined into nature. They even called Holy Spirit the Wild Goose!

In this story, St. Cuthbert was in a very remote place, journeying to reach isolated people with the Gospel. We call this 'wild wandering'. Following the unknown path. Cuthbert's young disciple was miserable due to hunger:

Cuthbert told him to cheer up and have faith: "The Lord will provide for us today. As he always does." He then pointed to an eagle flying high overhead. "See the bird flying high above us. It is possible for God to refresh us by ministrations of the eagle." The young man was not sure what Cuthbert was suggesting. But as they travelled further along the river, they saw the eagle settled on the bank with a fish in its claws. Cuthbert said, "Run and see what food the eagle has brought us from the Lord." This the young man did,

bringing back a large fish that the eagle had taken from the river. But Cuthbert said, "What have you done my son? Why have you not given our handmaiden her share? Cut it quickly in half and take her the share which she deserves for ministering to us."[4]

The Celts respected creation and understood our sacred connection.

Nature miracles continued throughout history. I could fill a book full of astonishing stories. Here's a more recent one, from author Mark Sandford's book; *Healing the Earth*. Mark was on a mission trip to Taiwan with his team. They had big problems with bug bites. Mark needed some urgent help:

Staff members complained that mosquitoes wouldn't let them sleep. Then I thought to myself, "Surely God's original intention for these creatures was not that they torment us! And if Jesus commanded the wind and the waves to be still, in His name I should at least be able to command mosquitoes not to bite." Not wanting to act presumptuously, I asked God for permission before commanding them in Jesus' name to stay away. The next morning I awakened unblemished from a dreamless sleep, while a baggy-eyed co-worker in the next room scratched his red blotches from head to toe.[5]

Perhaps Mark should have prayed for the whole team! Ha! We still have so much to learn. But we are growing and I think we will be amazed at how far this will actually go. We need to dream big!

Interestingly, the hebraic *Book of Jubilees*[6] teaches that animals were able to talk to mankind and each other back in the Beginning. They spoke with one voice. Tragically, the *Book of Jubilees* records this ability was lost at the fall. When Adam fell, they fell.

Yet in our "KAINOS" nature, I believe we can again make the language connection to animals. Our senses can be awakened:

But now ask the beasts, and they will teach you;
And the birds of the air, and they will tell you;
Or speak to the earth, and it will teach you;
And the fish of the sea will explain to you. (Job 12:7-8)

One day, I am certain, animals will also be restored back to their original design and right relationship with us. They are big part of the emerging transformed Earth. Kids will play with snakes and lions will eat straw (see Is 11:7-9 and 65:25). Amazing!

We have to recover the ALL of the Gospel. Jesus came to save what was lost, that includes the Earth, plants and the animals.

God was in Christ. He was working through Christ to bring the WHOLE WORLD back to Himself (Cor 5:19, NLV). God put the world square with himself through the Messiah, giving the WORLD a fresh start... (2 Cor 5:19, MSG).

St. Maximos understood we are connected to the future of the Universe:

Man is not a being isolated from the rest of creation; by his very nature he is bound with the whole of the universe... in his way to union with God, man in no way leaves creatures aside, but gathers in His love the whole cosmos disordered by sin, that it may be transfigured by grace.[7]

That is beautiful! Transfigured by grace! I love that phrase. Pure sweetness!

As we awaken, Earth will blossom and visibly respond. It will come alive!

"For you shall go out with joy, and be led out with peace; the mountains and the hills shall break forth into singing before you, and all the trees of the field shall clap *their* hands" (Is 55:12).

As we hold creation in our hearts we will find it is alive and ready to respond!

The challenge is to change our relationship with nature. This is a NOW word. It will make the difference between order and chaos, rains or drought, storms or calm.

We are the 'Guardians of the Earth'!

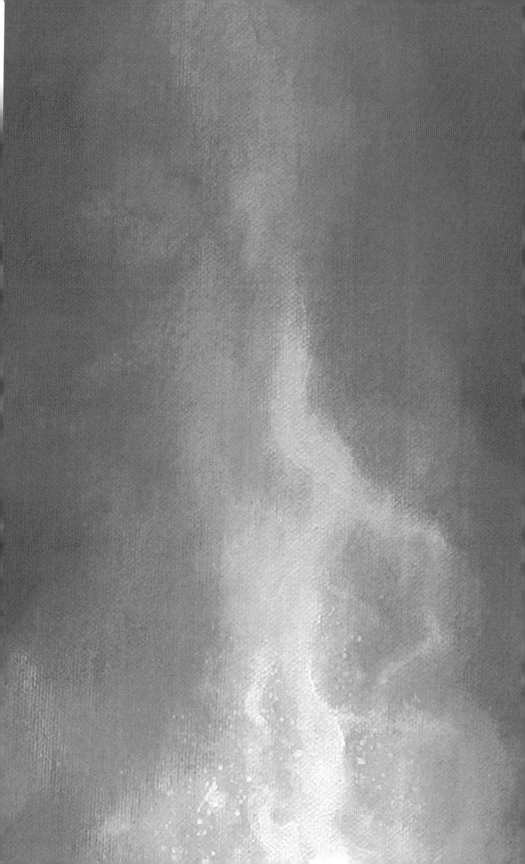

THE CELESTIAL CONFLICT

Then there was war in heaven: Michael and his angels fought the dragon. The dragon and his angels fought back (Rev 12:7, CEB).

We are nearing the end of this book. I hope you have enjoyed it so far. In the next two chapters I want to help prepare you for the fight ahead. In our joy we also need to be strong in the power of His might. Yes there is a battle, but Jesus said:

These things I have spoken to you, that in Me you may have peace. In the world you will have tribulation; but be of good cheer, I have overcome the world (John 16:33).

The truth is we are born-again into a celestial conflict, a battle that has raged since before Adam was ever created. A battle that devastated the cosmos and reduced the solar system to a shadow of what once existed.

Out of this chaotic mess God chose a tiny insignificant place to begin the process of re-creation. A place that has become pivotal to the future of all created things: Earth.

Adam was planted into a war-zone!

We know what happened next. Mankind fell and chaos again prevailed. Plants and animals became wild. The natural order of peace was subdued by survival and competition. Satan once again sat on top of his tiny mountain. Overconfident and proud.

Other celestial beings inspired by satanic pride joined the Earth rebellion. They were called the Watchers. Some people called them angels or gods. It is unclear where they came from. What we do know is that they left their allocated dimension and came to Earth, in direct opposition to the will of God. They taught people technology and occultic arts. Their story is told in the Ethiopic Book of Enoch.

Look and see what Azazel (the Watcher) has done to the earth - he has taught unrighteousness and has revealed eternal secrets that were once the preserve of heaven... In fact all of them have gone and 'slept' with human women and defiled themselves sexually and taught the people all kinds of sins. Each woman has given birth to an oversized giant in stature. Now they have gone wrong and killed many, spilling blood upon the ground and there is much unrighteousness.[1]

This accumulated in the time of Noah with one hell of a mess. Earth was ravished by demonic forces, mixed DNA beings, mighty ones and cannibalistic giants. Everywhere mankind had turned to complete lawlessness, the occult and perpetual evil.

When the Lord saw how great the wickedness of human beings was on earth, and how every desire that their heart conceived was always nothing but evil, the Lord regretted making human beings on the earth, and his heart was grieved (Gen 6:5).

At this point Earth was flooded. Some believe there may have been six billion people on Earth at the time with mixed DNA and sophisticated technology. The only survivors were Noah and his family. They escaped through Divine intervention.

It's mind-boggling to think Jesus said his return would be marked by a generation like that in the days of Noah. Stunning when you read Enoch and understand the times they were living in. Times of great conflict between light and darkness.

Jesus' hebraic audience were well familiar with the Book of Enoch and the ancient stories. They knew the implications. They knew it meant crazy days were coming!

As we grow in wisdom and spend time in the glory, Heaven begins to mentor us and teach us about this hidden conflict. The veil is peeled back and we begin to see there is more to this world than meets the eye.

In 2003 my eyes were unexpectedly opened. It began with a series of dreams.

I was shown a number of future events in detail. I saw the economic depression of the last decade. The spread of Islamic sharia law into the West. Legalisation of cannabis and many other drugs by the government. Gay marriage followed by group marriage. I was also shown how pornography would creep into mainstream media and even aim to captivate children. I saw many other things. Including agendas to have a counterfeit Islamic revival, and a westernised version of Islam that would impact fashion and celebrity culture. I couldn't continue as if everything was okay anymore. It wasn't!

I am still urged by these experiences to sound the alarm. I hate the apathy and complacency of our junk TV culture. We are on cruise control. I believe there is something more for our lives. I feel it and I can't live without it. There is more!

Respected prophet Paul Keith Davis has also had many profound visions and dreams about this critical era. Sitting in bed one night, he fell into some kind of visionary trance:

In this experience I saw hell. I was looking down into hell. I could see some invisible force... remove what looked like a man hole covering. I saw this big iron round gate into the bowels of hell. I called it the bowels of hell in the experience. I said something like 'Someone stop it!' I was screaming for someone to put the lid back on.

I saw evil spirits coming out of there just billowing out... I actually recognised the appearance of some. I saw what looked like the appearance of Adolf Hitler and Joseph Stalin and other tyrants,

people that were demonically anointed. I saw them coming up out of hell.

Somehow I was allowed to see these spirits manifesting themselves in a very real and visible way to people in their bedrooms... whether it was in dreams or in experiences I saw this evil of a different calibre of anything we have seen before. They began to manifest in these people's rooms. I saw them training these people how to walk in realms of darkness greater than we have ever seen.

Look at the news and I'd suggest this has already begun. Who would have thought groups like ISIS in Syria and Iraq would do such dark inhuman acts and broadcast it around the world? The videos and stories are unbelievable. Shocking!

Paul Keith continues:

When it was almost too much to bear, I said, "I can't watch this anymore!" I heard a voice come booming out of Heaven and say, "The sons of Light must respond in like manner." I saw these angels coming out of Heaven... These are angels that have been reserved for the end time confrontation. They have been standing in the presence of Almighty God... I saw these angels coming out of Heaven and manifesting themselves in people's bedrooms... I saw them training individuals how to walk in realms of glory, how to access the Spirit realm, how to be like John when he said "I was in the Spirit on the Lord's Day." John knew something! The secret of how to get in the Spirit.[2]

Don't you want that?

I recently had a significant vision-dream about this battle. It was like I was in a 3D movie! Demonic forces were fighting us on a mountain top. They looked like the ugly orc army in Lord of the Rings. They fought so hard it was unreal. We were in the thick of the fight. Clashing violently. It was full-on!

Then the view soared up higher like an eagle. I saw why it was so crazy.

I saw the orcs were at the top of the mountain and fully surrounded. It was their last stand. They were in sheer terror and panic. They had nowhere else to run. Nowhere to hide. They were fighting for their very existence.

Then I heard an audible voice shout across the battle field "It's time to SURGE!" I saw in the vision that if the forces of Light pushed together it would all be over quickly. If we converged and moved as one, the battle was done! I later found out the word 'surge' means: "a strong, wavelike, forward movement." This is what has to happen.

Our friend Ian Clayton thrives on the fight. He's not afraid of the demonic and has engaged them in conflict and won many times. He joyfully calls it "Shredding!" In our UK conference, Ian said this:

Our big problem is that what we have predominately (in the life of the Church) been teaching people about salvation. Teaching them and empowering them to live a life on Earth. Predominately that is what goes on in church life.

My biggest problem is that the only way you can (truly) live life on the Earth is to understand the life in the heavens. Because whatever goes on in the heavens has total dominion and influence over whatever goes on, on the face of the Earth.

Whatever goes on in the realm of the spirit changes what goes on in the face of the Earth. Whatever influences go on up there dictate what happens on the face of the Earth.

Until we learn that we are supposed to rule in those places and take our positions we are going to continue to get a fallen nature residing in the face of the Earth.[3]

The new world isn't coming without resistance. That battle is won or lost in multiple dimensions of existence seen and unseen. It's time to learn the ways of Heaven. To be about our Father's business which is righteousness, peace and joy!

(Jesus said) I saw Satan fall, a bolt of lightning out of the sky. See what I've given you? Safe passage as you walk on snakes and scorpions, and protection from every assault of the Enemy. No one can put a hand on you (Luke 10:19, MSG).

The glory of the Gospel, is that God now lives in us, and through us in victory. We now participate in the joy of justice. The joy of destroying the works of darkness. Evil forces are now far below us in Christ. They are limited in power. Put simply, Light wins!

Jesus is the example. He crushed and humiliated the enemy.

He stripped all the spiritual tyrants in the universe of their sham authority at the cross and marched them naked through the streets (Col 2:15, MSG).

We should follow his example. Haven't you had enough of being pushed around? As Bill Johnson says:

Satan is limited in every way. God gave him his gifts and abilities at his own creation. There has never been a battle between God and satan. The entire realm of darkness could be forever wiped out with a word. But God chose to defeat him through those made in His own likeness - those who would worship God by choice.[4]

We are the ones who are empowered to shape the future. If the world is a mess it is because we are not getting the Gospel yet. We have not fully understood that:

Jesus' primary mission is summed up in this one line: "For this purpose the Son of God was manifested, that He might destroy the works of the devil" (1 John 3:8). That was Jesus' assignment; it was the disciples' assignment and it is your assignment as well. God's purpose in saving you was not simply to rescue you and keep you busy until He shipped you off to Heaven. His purpose was much bigger; He commissioned you to demonstrate the will of God, "on earth as it is in heaven," helping to transform this planet into a place that is radiant and saturated with His power and

presence. This is the very backbone of the Great Commission, and it should define your life and mine.[5]

As UK prophetic song writer Godfrey Birtill says:

Enough - is enough - is enough - is enough!![6]

It's pay-back time! Can you feel it in the Spirit?

Our generation was wired for combat. Wired for victory.

Your people will offer themselves willingly [to participate in Your battle] in the day of Your power (Psalms 110:3, AMP).

There's a great battle coming. Don't fear. God lives in you!

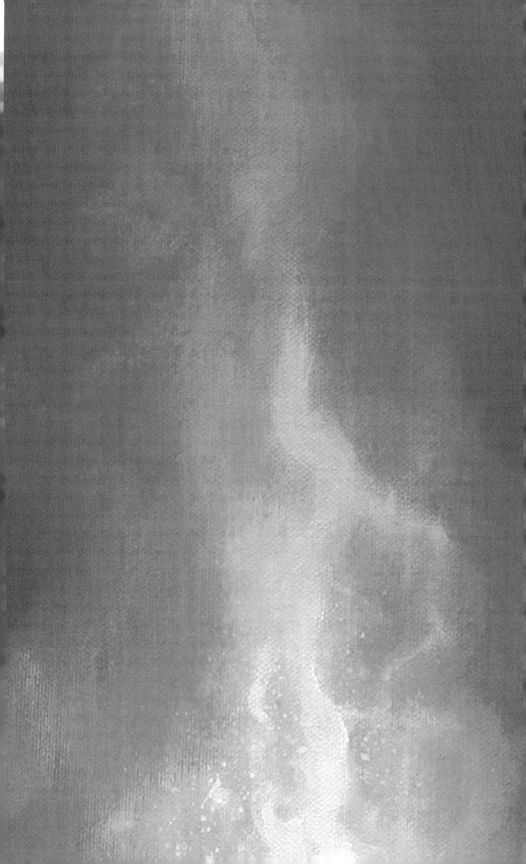

ENGAGING POWERS

For we are not struggling against human beings, but against the rulers, authorities and cosmic powers (Eph 6:12).

In the last chapter, we realised the "KAINOS" world isn't coming without a fight and this generation is up for it! We have Justice burning in our blood and faith bursting from our hearts. The Cross has condemned us to victory! It is inevitable!

Like dawn light moving over the mountains, a huge army is coming. There's never been anything like it and never will be again... Undaunted and fearless, unswerving, unstoppable (Joel 2, MSG).

You ready? I want to help you. Let's look at some real combat spiritual situations. Fill in some of the blanks. Remember our battle is not a human war nor limited to this physical world.

We're not waging war against enemies of flesh and blood alone. No, this fight is against tyrants, against authorities, against supernatural powers and demon princes that slither in the darkness of this world, and against wicked spiritual armies that lurk about in heavenly places. (Eph 6:12, VOI).

To talk about this, we're going to have to get a little weird.

Let's be honest. If you live in the Spirit you're going to see some really, really weird stuff. Some people claim it's all mythical, it's all made up. They are seriously wrong! It's real.

Something else appeared in the sky. It was a huge red dragon with seven heads and ten horns, and a crown on each of its seven heads (Rev 12:3, CEV).

Reading the book of Revelation is like going on a wild fantasy ride. It's crazy!

I heard the voice of the fourth living creature saying, "Come and see." So I looked, and behold, a pale horse. And the name of him who sat on it was Death, and Hades followed with him (Rev 6:7).

If you get freaked out easily, maybe this chapter isn't right for you yet. Come back to it.

I'm just going to be honest. I never went looking for any of it. I pursued God. Spent years soaking in the presence. Gradually I saw more about how the world functions.

We had to slowly learn to deal with the junk. Strange entities such as dragons, transdimensional creatures, water spirits, demonic possession, storms, dark orbs, things that look like skinny tall ogres, even human witches. The battle came to us!

In the physical we have been mobbed by angry crowds. Seen religious people burning red with anger. Nearly been arrested on the streets. Someone tried to kill me in a youth meeting in France. All stirred up by demonic powers. This stuff is real!

The Earth has a lot of junk in it. It's just the way it is right now.

Until the restoration of all things, we have a battle to fight and a world to transform. If you want to occupy the mountains you have to kick off any false gods that may be there. It's just the way it is.

These dark forces have resisted Heaven for eons. They are overconfident and prideful. Convinced they will hold the ground. I have visited a 'Cabal' in the Spirit. They are the most arrogant, self-assured beings you can imagine. I can't tell you how full of pride they are. Smartly dressed, selfish and pompous. Feeding off the dust of mankind.

It's going to be glorious seeing the end of their era! Can you imagine it?!

To understand how to win the war, we must look at Jesus again. Jesus was led by the Spirit into combat. It is actually God himself who sets us up for victory.

Now Jesus, full of the Holy Spirit, left the Jordan and was led by the Spirit into the wild. For forty wilderness days and nights he was tested by the Devil (Luke 4:1, MSG).

This is the place of ultimate safety and joy. Living in the Spirit. Maturity is being led.

For all who are led by the Spirit of God are the (mature) sons of God (Rom 8:14).

So what happened next? Prophetic writer Rick Joyner has an idea. Rick was shown in a series of experiences what happened. He records it in *When God walked the Earth.*[1]

Jesus walked into the desert under a cloud of darkness such as had never been witnessed on the earth before. Demons of every kind were swarming through the mid-heavens all around and above the wilderness.

Rick saw demonic hordes swirl around the region bringing heaviness and depression to the area. Stirring up discord and storms. Eventually Satan appeared. He had one goal, to seduce Jesus into moving apart from the Father's will.

Lucifer stood in his most glorious apparel - more stunning than any earthly king could have ever imagined. His face was so kind and appealing, any child would have easily come to him. Jesus knew him immediately and stood to his feet to face him.

Jesus was not moved by appearance or seduction. He remained humbly obedient to the Father. Anchored in his love. Willing to suffer for the sake of humanity. He saw something in us worth laying down his life for. He saw what we would become. His Bride.

I love what Rick saw next. It's beautiful. Overjoyed at the victory, Michael and the angels lined the wilderness to comfort and honour him. The skies opened.

For a thousand miles in every direction the sky glistened with the swords of the angelic hosts that were drawn to salute him. In Heaven the glory of the celebration was greater than had ever been witnessed before. Every angel, every cherubim, every created being in Heaven, sang, danced, and rejoiced with all that was within them. Truth was victorious!

As Jesus began to walk along the dusty road from the wilderness, He could now feel the delight of the Father. All of the angels who lined the road, with their swords drawn in salute as they bowed on one knee, could also feel the Father's delight. This was the food of angels. Hours before it had been the darkest of times, and now it was the brightest. How quickly it had all changed!

I love that. Take encouragement friend, if you are also in a time of trial. Hold fast. The storm will break. God is faithful and will see you through, with much joy and honour!

Weeping may endure for a night, but joy comes in the morning (Psalms 30:5).

Following Christ, the early church won massive territories. The 120 were unstoppable. The more darkness resisted, the greater the expansion. Even martyrdom seeded the fire, and it spread throughout the Roman world within a generation.

Rejecting the corruption of Rome, courageous small communities emerged. They were the "Desert Fathers". Perhaps you've heard about them? In the desert they found Eden.

One of the first was St. Antony of Egypt[2]. He gave himself to deep prayer and fasting. In his humble home, alone, Antony pressed through extreme demonic battles.

There was a sudden noise which caused the place to shake violently: holes appeared in the walls and a horde of different kinds of demons poured out. They took the shapes of wild animals and snakes and instantly filled the whole place with spectres in the form of lions, bulls, wolves, vipers, serpents, scorpions and even leopards and bears, too. They all made noises according to their individual nature... The face of each of them bore a savage expression and the sound of their fierce voices were terrifying.

Antony, beaten and mauled... remained unafraid, his mind alert... though the wounds of his flesh made him groan, he maintained the same attitude and spoke as if mocking his enemies "If you have any influence, if the Lord has granted power over me, look, here I am: devour me. But if you cannot, why do you expend so much useless effort? For the sign of the cross and faith in the Lord is for us a wall that no assault of yours can break down."

Despite the big show, the enemy is limited. The cross has already won every battle. The dear saint, moved by Love continued to pray the Psalms. Looking to Jesus.

Antony raised his eyes, he saw the roof opening above him and, as the darkness was dispelled, a ray of light poured in on him. As soon as this bright light appeared, all the demons vanished and the pain in Antony's body suddenly ceased. Furthermore the building which had been destroyed a moment earlier was restored. Antony immediately understood the Lord was present. Sighing deeply from the bottom of his heart, he addressed the light that had appeared to him, saying, 'Where were you, good Jesus? Where were you? Why were you not here from the beginning to heal my wounds?' And a voice came to him saying, 'Antony, I was here, but I was waiting to watch your struggle. But now, since you have bravely held your own in this fight, I will always help you and I will make you famous throughout the earth... Antony was thirty five years old at the time.

Jesus was true to his word. Antony's little life had big ripples. Inspired countless people to form monastic prayer communities. The Celtic saints, the Franciscans, and many others were inspired by his example. Even Rome sought his council.

In fact, Satan was so crushed by Antony, he came to his house, knocked on the door and begged him to stop. It's incredible! Satan (in the form of a monk) said:

I am to be pitied. I ask you, have you not read, the enemy's swords are broken forever and you have destroyed their cities. Look I have no place to be now; I possess no city; I have no weapons now. Throughout every nation and all the province the name of Jesus rings out and even the desert is crammed full with monks.

No wonder God laughs at him (Psalms 2:4). Can you see how humiliated he is by Jesus? I'll let Antony tell you what happened next.

Then I marvelled and rejoiced at God's grace and addressed the demon with these words: "For although you are a master of deceit, you have been forced to admit this without lying. Truly Jesus has utterly destroyed your powers, stripped you of your honours as an angel, you lie rolling in the mud." I had hardly finished speaking when this tall figure collapsed at the mention of the Saviour's name.

Why did I chose this story? Because you may be going through a fight right now. Warfare is not a sign you are off-track. It seems to come more powerfully on the pathway of destiny. Hold fast and press into Jesus. You have been called for greatness.

Maybe this is all too much for you to handle? Don't worry! I have found Jesus grows you into the fight gradually as your trust and faith in him grows. He is the Good Shepherd who cares for his sheep.

You spread out a table before me, provisions in the midst of attack from my enemies; You care for all my needs, anointing my head with soothing, fragrant oil, filling my cup again and again with Your

grace (Psalms 23:5, VOI).

Rest is the greatest weapon we have. When we rest in Him, He rests in us and we are complete. This is the ultimate victory, sitting with Him on His throne.

To him who overcomes I will grant to sit with Me on My throne, as I also overcame and sat down with My Father on His throne (Rev 3:21).

I hope some of this chapter has been helpful. There is so much more to say, but I'm confident Jesus will teach you all you need to know from here. You're in safe hands!

We will end here with this brilliant quote from "Lord of the Rings". A story where tiny folk called hobbits, with their heroic ragtag friends overcome the greatest darkness of all.

It's like in the great stories, Mr. Frodo. The ones that really mattered. Full of darkness and danger they were. And sometimes you didn't want to know the end. Because how could the end be happy? How could the world go back to the way it was when so much bad had happened? But in the end, it's only a passing thing, this shadow. Even darkness must pass. A new day will come. And when the sun shines it will shine out the clearer.[3]

I love happy endings!

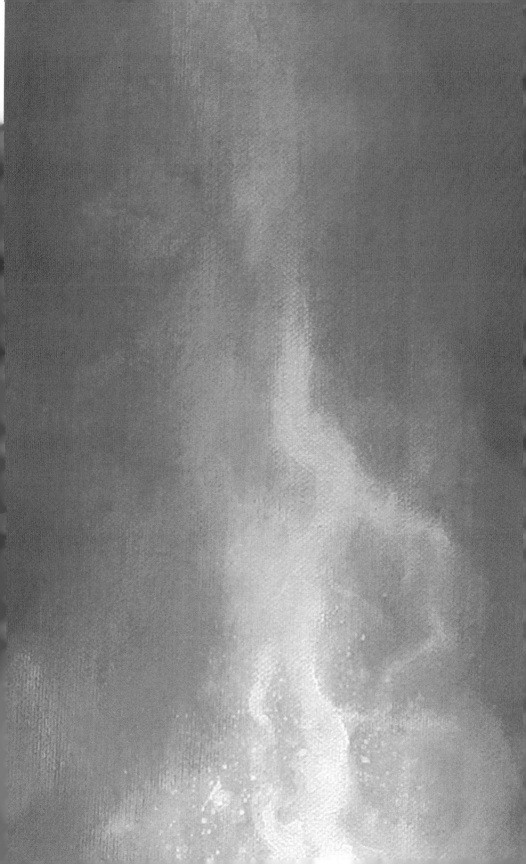

EPILOGUE:
BEYOND EARTH
THE COSMIC
IMPLICATIONS

I couldn't end this book without teasing you with one last mystery.
A mystery I've been contemplating for years. This is a fun future-gazing
idea to stretch you at the end. Let's talk about living "Beyond Earth:
The Cosmic implications of the Gospel"!

I love the Earth. It is the cradle of humanity. As great as it is now, we
know it will be changed into something far more wonderful. It will be
made gloriously brand new again.

**Now I saw a new Heaven and a new Earth, for the first Heaven
and the first earth had passed away. Also there was no more sea.
Then I, John, saw the holy city, New Jerusalem, coming down
out of Heaven from God, prepared as a bride adorned for her
husband. And I heard a loud voice from Heaven saying, "Behold,
the tabernacle of God is with men, and He will dwell with them,
and they shall be His people. God Himself will be with them and be
their God." (Rev 21:1-3).**

Thrusting us into a golden age. We will see God. Everything will change.

Yet here again is another "KAINOS" age mystery. Something very close
to the Father's heart. It is the role of the Ecclesia in governing the entire
cosmos. We are co-heirs with Christ, of all that belongs to the Father.

The Spirit Himself bears witness with our spirit that we are children of God, and if children, then heirs - heirs of God and joint heirs with Christ (Rom 8:16-17).

ALL that Christ claims as His will belong to all of us as well (PHI).

You are powerful to think differently, but follow the logic of the glorious Gospel:

For [even the whole] creation (all nature) waits expectantly and longs earnestly for God's sons to be made known [waits for the revealing, the disclosing of their sonship] (Rom 8:19, AMPC).

And the hope is that in the end the whole of created life will be rescued from the tyranny of change and decay, and have its share in that magnificent liberty which can only belong to the children of God (Rom 8:18-21, CEB)!

Think about that, everything, everywhere, waits to be freed from decay by the children of Light. Don't miss the profound implications hidden in the Word. The Bible is incredible. It does not hold back to what we are comfortable with. It invites us into the beauty of mystery. Invites us to places beyond our wildest dreams.

God can do anything, you know - far more than you could ever imagine or guess or request in your wildest dreams! (Eph 3:20, MSG).

Can we just talk about space for a moment? Our planet is floating in space. We see the stars and moon at night. Space is a vital part of our life.

Look into space, there are at least 13.8 billion light years of cosmos just in this known universe, full of galaxies, each with billions of stars, planets and moons. It's beautiful.

Scientists say if you put a single pin hole in the night sky there are approximately 10,000 galaxies just in that one area. Can you imagine that? One pin hole is 10,000 galaxies!

What's in those galaxies? Does the "KAINOS" creation have a purpose beyond Earth, amongst the stars? Do you ever think about this? I never used to. Yet in South Africa in 2013, I saw a revelatory book being unlocked in a dream. I saw sealed up truth now being revealed to many. Holy Spirit is awakening us to new glorious possibilities:

Yet to us God has unveiled and revealed them by *and* through His [Holy] Spirit, for the [Holy] Spirit searches diligently, exploring *and* examining everything, even sounding the profound and bottomless things of God [the divine counsels and things hidden and beyond man's scrutiny] (1 Cor 2:10-12, AMPC).

We used to think space was mostly black and empty. Science is discovering it is more beautiful and wonderful than we ever imagined in the past. Space is full of giant stars, black holes, whirling nebulas, beautiful colours and black matter (the mysterious substance that accounts for most of the universe). We know so little.

Scientists used to think Earth was the only planet suitable for life. Now they are finding many possible planets in the habitable zone around stars. Senior astronomer Seth Shostak of the SETI Institute (search for extraterrestrial intelligence) says:

The number of habitable worlds in our galaxy is certainly in the tens of billions, minimum, and we haven't even talked about the moons. You know, moons can be habitable, too. And the number of galaxies we can see, other than our own, is about 100 billion. So 100 billion times 10 billion is a thousand billion billion [habitable planets] in the visible universe.[1]

All this is within our bubble of space called the uni-verse. There may be more out there.

The universe we live in may not be the only one out there. In fact, our universe could be just one of an infinite number of universes making up a "multiverse."[2]

Scripture teaches God made many "heavenly" places.

In the beginning God created the HEAVENS and the earth (Gen 1:1).

'Heavens' in Bible talk can also sometimes mean 'Space'. Look again at these verses:

I consider Your heavens, the work of Your fingers,
The moon and the stars, which You have ordained (Psalms 8:3).

Then He brought him outside and said, "Look now toward heaven, and count the stars if you are able to number them." And He said to him, "So shall your descendants be." (Gen 15:5).

And take heed, lest you lift your eyes to heaven, and when you see the sun, the moon, and the stars, all the host of heaven, you feel driven to worship them and serve them (Deut 4:9).

There are certainly other dimensions right beside us now:

There is an unseen realm (2 Cor 4:18), third heaven (2 Cor 12:2), heaven of heavens (2 Chron 6:18), many mansions in the house (John 14:2), places on the Earth and under the Earth (Rev 5:3), within the Sun (Rev 19:7) and hades or hell (Luke 16:23).

Quantum string theorists suggest there are ten dimensions. Most of them beyond the present ability of science to discover. Other quantum theorists say there could be even more. I once heard Ian Clayton say there are 32! I've not asked him about it yet.

This is the more amazing wonder: somehow all of it, every-thing is waiting for Jesus to be revealed in the "KAINOS" sons. It is waiting for our revealing with Christ in glory.

The whole creation is on tiptoe to see the wonderful sight of the sons of God coming into their own (CEB) ...can hardly wait for what's coming next (MSG).

[The purpose is] that through the church the complicated, many-sided wisdom of God in all its infinite variety and innumerable aspects might now be made known to the angelic rulers and authorities (principalities and powers) in the heavenly sphere (Eph 3:10, AMP).

It is written in our spiritual DNA to go further out just like Enoch the friend of God.

Enoch saw "all the secrets of heavens" and was the first to write about the Solar System. This is recorded in the Ethiopic Book of Enoch[3] which Jude also quoted from in the New Testament. Enoch was the seventh from Adam, which is symbolic of the end of this age.

I want to suggest that Earth is just the beginning of re-creation. It is the cradle of humanity, the start of a wonder-filled journey of spreading Heaven's blissful order into the chaos, reconciling it back to Christ, bringing it back to the beauty of the Design.

His ever-expanding, peaceful government will never end. He will rule with perfect fairness and justice from the throne of his father David (TLB). His dominion will grow continually, and to peace there will be no end (LEB). It will have... unlimited growth (GW) (Is 9:7).

We presume all of this is just for the future. However, Rick Joyner believes some of the saints in Heaven are already learning to govern cosmic places. In his excellent book *The Final Quest* Rick wrote what he saw in a heavenly vision:

As I approached the Judgment Seat of Christ, those in the highest ranks were also sitting on thrones that were all a part of His throne. Even the least of these thrones was more glorious than any earthly throne many times over. Some of these were rulers over the affairs of Heaven, and others over the affairs of the physical creation, such as star systems and galaxies.[4]

I think most of the people who read that profound book overlooked the implications of what Rick Joyner saw. Perhaps we are now ready to truly listen? God is breaking the box!

One time I was deeply absorbed in God, praying with friends. Suddenly I saw a very bright light. For a few seconds I was pulled quickly upwards within this beam. I had the sensation of moving at great speed.

Without warning I found myself with Jesus in another part of space. We were both standing on what looked like a moon facing a beautiful nebula. It was wonderful!

There were angels as balls of living light moving in and out of the nebula clouds worshiping God. The dust clouds were vibrant with reds and oranges. There was a stunning blueish planet nearby with rings like Saturn. It filled most of the sky. It was breathtaking!

After a very short time, I was pulled back without warning into the prayer room, full of the Holy Spirit, wondering why this had happened. I think like all great artists, Jesus wanted to show me a little of what He made. It was all created by Him and for Him. The amazing thing, He loves to share His creation with us! He loves us!

For by Him all things were created that are in heaven and that are on earth, visible and invisible, whether thrones or dominions or principalities or powers. All things were created through Him and for Him (Col 1:16).

Jesus made it all. We should not be afraid of it. It is part of His life and now ours as those joined with Him in union. I know this is all a bit different from what we're used to talking about. As you grow up you find out more. It is by Divine Design!

In conclusion, in all I have written in this book, I firmly believe what is coming has no historic precedent. It is not just a repeat of past revivals or outpourings (as much as we love and honour the past). No mind-box can contain the limitless Christ in us.

The apostle Paul understood this truth and said:

I never give up praying for you; and this is my prayer. That God, the God of our Lord Jesus Christ and the all-glorious Father, will give you spiritual wisdom and the insight to know more of him: that you may receive that inner illumination of the spirit which will make you realise how great is the hope to which he is calling you - the magnificence and splendour of the inheritance promised to Christians - and how tremendous is the power available to us who believe in God (Eph 1:17-19, PHI).

We are going
interstellar
transdimensional
and immortal.

Whatever comes in the future will involve the cosmos. Whether through advancing space and quantum technology, "KAINOS" teleportation or simply learning to move more fully in the Spirit Realm beyond our bodies, I know we are growing up into a much bigger picture. God is leading us into a brand new world and we will never look back!

The final generations on this earth are going to live the greatest adventure the world has ever known.[5]

Truly, we will say God saved the best wine until last!

BIBLE TRANSLATIONS

Unless otherwise stated, I have used the New King James Version (NKJV, Copyright © 1982 by Thomas Nelson) for the Bible quotes in this book. The additional translations I've used are as follows:

AMP - Amplified Bible Copyright © 2015 by The Lockman Foundation, La Habra, CA 90631

AMPC - Amplified Bible, Classic Edition Copyright © 1954, 1958, 1962, 1964, 1965, 1987 by The Lockman Foundation

BE - Bible in Basic English, Copyright © 1965 by Cambridge Press in England

CEV - Contemporary English Version, Copyright © 1995 by American Bible Society

CJB - Complete Jewish Bible, Copyright © 1998 by David H. Stern

DAR - Darby Translation, Public Domain

DLNT - Disciples' Literal New Testament, Copyright © 2011 Michael J. Magill. All Rights Reserved. Published by Reyma Publishing

DRB - Douay-Rheims 1899 American Edition, Public Domain

ERV - Easy-to-Read Version, Copyright © 2006 by Bible League International

GW - GOD'S WORD Translation Copyright © 1995 by God's Word to the Nations. Baker Publishing Group

HCSB - Holman Christian Standard Bible, Copyright © 1999, 2000, 2002, 2003, 2009 by Holman Bible Publishers, Nashville Tennessee.

ISV - International Standard Version, Copyright © 1995-2014 by ISV Foundation. Davidson Press, LLC.

KJV - King James Version, Public Domain

KNO – The New Testament Paperback, Copyright © 1997 by Ronald A. Knox.

LEB - Lexham English Bible 2012 by Logos Bible Software. Lexham is a registered trademark of Logos Bible Software

MIR - The Mirror Bible, Copyright © 2012 by Francois du Toit.

MSG - The Message (MSG) Copyright © 1993, 1994, 1995, 1996, 2000, 2001, 2002 by Eugene H. Peterson

NLT - New Living Translation, Copyright© 1996, 2004, 2007, 2013 by Tyndale House Foundation. Tyndale House Publishers Inc., Carol Stream, Illinois 60188. All rights reserved.

NLV - New Life Version, Copyright © 1969 by Christian Literature International

NOG - Names of God Bible, The Names of God Bible (without notes) Copyright © 2011 by Baker Publishing Group.

PAS - The Passion Translation Copyright © 2014, by Brian Simmons

PHI - The New Testament in Modern English by J.B Philips copyright © 1960, 1972 J. B. Phillips. Administered by The Archbishops' Council of the Church of England.

TLB - The Living Bible copyright © 1971 by Tyndale House Foundation

TCNT -Twentieth Century New Testament, Copyright © 2013 by Hardpress Publishing.

WE - Worldwide English (New Testament) Copyright © 1969, 1971, 1996, 1998 by SOON Educational Publications

WMS - The New Testament in the Language of the People Translated from the Greek by Charles B. Williams, Copyright © 1972 Moody Publishers

WNT - The Weymouth New Testament (also known as The New Testament in Modern Speech) Copyright © 1903, James Clarke & Co (London)

VOI - The Voice, The Voice Bible Copyright © 2012 Thomas Nelson, Inc. The Voice™ translation © 2012 Ecclesia Bible Society

REFERENCES

Prologue: The Dawn
(1) Larry Randolph, *Spirit Talk, Hearing the Voice of God*. MorningStar Publications (2005).
(2) C. S. Lewis, *Mere Christianity*. Quote accessed via www.goodreads.com
(3) Rick Joyner, *A Prophetic Vision for the 21st Century*. Thomas Nelson Publishers, 1999.
(4) Patricia King, *Spiritual Revolution: Experience the Supernatural in Your Life*. Destiny Image (2006).

Part One - Introduction
The Coming Harvest
(1) Rick Joyner, *Visions of the Harvest - Updated and Expanded*. E-Book Edition. Distributed by MorningStar Publications, Inc (2013).

The "KAINOS" Sons
(1) James Strong. *Strong's Biblical Dictionary* published in 1800. Accessed online via www.blueletterbible.org.
(2) W.E. Vine's M.A., *Expository Dictionary of New Testament Words* published in 1940 and without copyright.

Mystical Co-Mission
(1) Patricia King, *Spiritual Revolution, Experience the Supernatural in Your Life Through Angelic Visitations, Prophetic Dreams, Visions, and Miracles*. Destiny Image (2006).
(2) Rick Joyner, find out more via www.morningstarministries.org.

Part Two - Beyond Human
Chapter 1 - Living from Zion
(1) Paul Keith Davis, find out more via www.whitedoveministries.org.
(2) Roland H. Buck, *Angels on Assignment*. Whitaker House (1979).
(3) Rick Joyner, *The Sword and the Torch*. Morningstar Publications (2003).
(4) James Maloney, *Ladies of Gold: The Remarkable Ministry of the Golden Candlestick*, Volume One: 1. Answering the Cry Publications (2011).
(5) Rick Joyner, *The Sword and the Torch*. Morningstar Publications (2003).
(6) Martin Luther King, Jr. quote from BrainyQuote.com.

(7) Ian Clayton's resources are available at www.sonofthunder.org.nz.

Chapter 2 - Angelic Community
(1) Bobby Connor, https://companyofburninghearts.wordpress.com/2011/10/14/other-voices-bobby-conner-wisdom/ (2011).
(2) Richard Sharpe, *Adomnan of Iona - Life of St Columba*. Penguin Books (1995).
(3) Randy Clark, *Kingdom Foundations* - a conference in Cardiff, Wales (2013).
(4) John Paul Jackson, quote taken from a live recording in England, UK. Find out more about John Paul at www.streamsministries.com.
(5) Roland H. Buck, *Angels on Assignment*. Whitaker House (1979).
(6) Gary Oates, *Open My Eyes, Lord: A Practical Guide to Angelic Visitations and Heavenly Experiences*. Open Heaven Publications (2004).

Chapter 3 - Cloud of Witnesses
(1) C. S. Lewis, via www.goodreads.com.
(2) Rick Joyner, *The Final Quest*. MorningStar Publications (1996).
(3) Roberts Liardon, *We Saw Heaven*. Destiny Image (2000).
(4) Godfrey Birtill, *Two Thousand Years Ago*. 2012 © Thankyou Music UK.
(5) James Innell Packer and Thomas C. Oden, *One Faith The Evangelical Consensus*. InterVarsity Press (2004).
(6) Rev. Fr. Angelo Pastrovicchi, *St. Joseph of Copertino*. TAN Books (1980).
(7) Saint Francis of Assisi, via www.goodreads.com.
(8) Paul Keith Davis, from a live conference teaching session. Find more Paul Keith teachings via www.whitedoveministries.org.

Chapter 4 - Telepathic by Design
(1) Upton Sinclair, *Mental Radio*. Read Books Ltd (2013).
(2) Hans Berger, quoted from http://news.discovery.com/human/life/love-telepathy-is-it-real-120212.htm.
(3) Quote accessed via http://www.spiritscienceandmetaphysics.com/scientific-proof-our-minds-are-all-connected/.
(4) Quote accessed via http://www.dailymail.co.uk/news/article-2745797/Scientists-claim-telepathy-success-sending-mental-message-one-person-4-000-miles-away.html.

Chapter 5 - Telepathic Hubs: One Body
(1) David Humphries, *The Lost Book of Enoch*. Cambridge Media Group (2006).
(2) Jan Johnson, *Madame Guyon*. Bethany House Publishers (1998).

(3) Joan Carroll Cruz. *Mysteries, Marvels, Miracles in the Lives of the Saints*. Tan Books and Publishers (1997).
(4) As above.

Chapter 6 - Remote Sight
(1) https://en.wikipedia.org/wiki/Remote_viewing
(2) Richard Sharpe, *Adomnan of Iona - Life of St Columba*. Penguin Books (1995).
(3) Lyrics available at: http://www.metrolyrics.com/a-whole-new-world-lyrics-aladdin.html

Chapter 7 - Infused Knowledge
(1) Definition of "Infused Knowledge" obtained from http://www.catholicculture.org/culture/library/dictionary/index.cfm?id=34207
(2) Kathie Walters, *Celtic Flames*. Good News Ministries (1999).
(3) John G. Lake, *John G. Lake: His Life, His Sermons, His Boldness of Faith*. Kenneth Copeland Publishing (1995).
(4) David Humphries, *The Lost Book of Enoch*. Cambridge Media Group (2006).

Chapter 8 - Miraculous Transports
(1) John Paul Jackson, quote taken from a live recording in England, UK. Find out more about John Paul at www.streamsministries.com.
(2) As above.
(3) Joan Carroll Cruz. *Mysteries, Marvels, Miracles in the Lives of the Saints*. Tan Books and Publishers (1997).
(4) As above.
(5) As above.
(6) You can find out more by listening to our FREE Podcast called "*Transrelocation with Ian Clayton*".
Available at http://companyofburninghearts.podomatic.com or iTunes.

Chapter 9 - Metamorphosis
(1) David Adam, *Walking the Edges, Living in the Presence of God*. Society for Promoting Christian Knowledge, Bookmarque Ltd (2003).
(2) Joan Carroll Cruz. *Mysteries, Marvels, Miracles in the Lives of the Saints*. Tan Books and Publishers (1997).
(3) Cassandra Eason, *Fabulous Creatures, Mythical Monsters, and Animal Power Symbols: A Handbook*. Greenwood Publishing Group (2008).
(4) Available FREE at: http://companyofburninghearts.podomatic.com.

Chapter 10 - Dimensional Shifts

(1) Julian of Norwich. Quote accessed via: http://jordandenari.com/2013/11/08/more-in-heaven-wisdom-from-julian-of-norwich/.

(2) Joan Carroll Cruz. *Mysteries, Marvels, Miracles in the Lives of the Saints*. Tan Books and Publishers (1997).

(3) As above.

(4) Brother Yun with Paul Hattaway, *The Heavenly Man: The Remarkable True Story Of Chinese Christian Brother Yun*. Monarch Books (2002).

(5) Michael Van Vlymen, *Supernatural Transportation, Moving Through Space, Time and Dimensions for the Kingdom of Heaven*. Ministry Resources (2016).

(6) Nancy Coen's teachings are available through Benji Fiordland at www.revivalschoolnz.com.

Chapter 11 - Inedia: Prolonged Fasting

(1) John Crowder, *The Ecstasy of Loving God: Trances, Raptures, and the Supernatural Pleasures of Jesus Christ*. Destiny Image (2008).

(2) Kathie Walters, *Celtic Flames*. Good News Ministries (1999).

(3) Brother Yun with Paul Hattaway, *The Heavenly Man: The Remarkable True Story Of Chinese Christian Brother Yun*. Monarch Books (2002).

(4) Joan Carroll Cruz. *Mysteries, Marvels, Miracles in the Lives of the Saints*. Tan Books and Publishers (1997).

(5) For more on this listen to our Podcast teaching - *Life and Immortality*. Available FREE at: http://companyofburninghearts.podomatic.com. (March 2015)

Chapter 12 - Beyond Sleep: Redeeming the Night

(1) Paul Keith Davis, speaking at the "Promised Land" workshop in Chester UK with MorningStar Europe (Nov 2015). Visit www.morningstareurope.org for more info.

(2) Nancy Coen's teachings are available through Benji Fiordl and at www.revivalschoolnz.com. Highly recommended!

(3) David Adam, *Aidan, Bede, Cuthbert: Three Inspirational Saints*. Society for Promoting Christian Knowledge, Bookmarque Ltd (2006).

(4) W. Heywood, *The Little Flowers of St. Francis of Assisi*. Arrow Books Ltd (1998).

(5) Montague Summers, *Physical Phenomena of Mysticism*. Kessinger Publishing Co (2003).

(6) James Strong. Strong's *Biblical Dictionary* published in 1800. Accessed online via www.blueletterbible.org.

Chapter 13 - Mastery over Creation

(1) John Paul Jackson. Quoted from: http://www.streamsministries.com/resources/discipleship/some-thoughts-about-the-earth-and-righteousness.
(2) Supernatural weather miracle - http://www.telegraph.co.uk/finance/newsbysector/retailandconsumer/8985975/Shops-feel-the-chill-as-country-basks-in-mild-winter.html.
(3) W. Heywood, *The Little Flowers of St. Francis of Assisi*. Arrow Books Ltd (1998).
(4) David Adam, *Aidan, Bede, Cuthbert: Three Inspirational Saints*. Society for Promoting Christian Knowledge, Bookmarque Ltd (2006).
(5) John Sandford and Mark Sandford, *Healing the Earth... A Time for Change*. BT Johnson Publishing (2013).
(6) R. H. Charles, *The Book of Jubilees. From "The Apocrypha and Pseudepigrapha of the Old Testament"*. Oxford Clarendon Press (1913).
(7) John Sandford and Mark Sandford, *Healing the Earth... A Time for Change*. BT Johnson Publishing (2013).

Chapter 14 - The Celestial Conflict

(1) David Humphries, *The Lost Book of Enoch*. Cambridge Media Group (2006).
(2) Paul Keith Davis, *The Days of Noah* audio teaching series. Available to purchase at www.whitedoveministries.org.
(3) Ian Clayton from a live teaching at *"Beyond the Veil"* with COBH. Find teaching resources at: www.sonofthunder.org.nz.
(4) Bill Johnson, *Hosting the Presence: Unveiling Heaven's Agenda*. Destiny Image (2012).
(5) Bill Johnson, *Spiritual Java*. Destiny Image (2010).
(6) Godfrey Birtill, *Hijacked into Paradise*. Whitefield Music (2009).

Chapter 15 - Engaging Powers

(1) Rick Joyner, *When God Walked the Earth*. MorningStar Publications (2007).
(2) Carolinne White, *Early Christian Lives*. Penguin Books (1998).
(3) J. R. R. Tolkien, via http://www.councilofelrond.com/moviebook/4-07-the-stories-that-really-matter/.

Epilogue: Beyond Earth - The Cosmic Implications

(1) Seth Shostak. Quoted from: http://www.huffingtonpost.com/2014/06/24/habitable-planets-seth-shostak_n_5527116.html.
(2) Clara Moskowitz. Quoted from: http://www.space.com/18811-multiple-universes-5-theories.html.
(3) David Humphries, *The Lost Book of Enoch*. Cambridge Media Group (2006).
(4) Rick Joyner, *The Final Quest*. MorningStar Publications (1996).

(5) Rick Joyner, *The Apostolic Ministry*. MorningStar Publications (2004).

Bonus Chapter: Walking on Air
(1) John Crowder, *The Ecstasy of Loving God, Trances, Raptures and the Supernatural Pleasures of Jesus Christ*. Destiny Image (2009).
(2) Teresa of Avila and J. Cohen, *The Life of Saint Teresa of Avila by Herself*. Penguin Books (1987).
(3) As above.
(4) Joan Carroll Cruz. *Mysteries, Marvels, Miracles in the Lives of the Saints*. Tan Books and Publishers (1997).
(5) Raymond of Capua, *The Life of St. Catherine of Sienna*. Public Domain.
(6) Joan Carroll Cruz. *Mysteries, Marvels, Miracles in the Lives of the Saints*. Tan Books and Publishers (1997).
(7) Rev. Fr. Angelo Pastrovicchi, *St. Joseph of Copertino*. TAN Books (1980).
(8) John G. Lake, *John G. Lake: His Life, His Sermons, His Boldness of Faith*. Kenneth Copeland Publishing (1995).

BONUS CHAPTER: WALKING ON AIR

Your vibrant beauty has gotten inside us - you've been so good to us! We're walking on air! (Psalms 89, MSG).

Ah you've found the secret chapter! Like an extra scene in the movie credits, I thought it would be fun to squeeze in one more "KAINOS" idea. I wrote a number of other chapters that didn't make the final cut, but I just couldn't leave this out. It's just too much "KAINOS" fun!!

LEVITATION!

If you still want a little more then read on... here we go!

Jesus came and restored us back to where we were always supposed to be. In His last act before returning to Heaven, He floated right off the ground and vanished.

As He finished this commission, He began to rise from the ground before their eyes until the clouds obscured Him from their vision (Acts 1:9, VOI).

I think Jesus did this to show the world, the sons own the skies. Whoever owns the skies wins the war.

Many have followed in Jesus' footsteps and floated upwards. Hundreds of Catholic saints have been seen doing this. And how many others have done this privately?

Who *are* these *who* fly like a cloud? (Is 60:8).

This miracle is called 'Levitation' or 'Ascension'. It is one of the phenomena of mystic prayer, most often associated with ecstasies and raptures.

It seems gravity is a lesser force than the ravishing updrafts of Divine Love!

Listen to this testimony of Maria Villani, a Dominican nun:

On one occasion I found myself conscious of a new experience. I felt myself seized and ravished out of my senses, and that so powerfully that I found myself lifted up completely by the soles of my feet, just as the magnet draws up a fragment of iron, but with gentleness that was marvellous and delightful. At first I felt much fear, but afterwards I remained in the greatest possible contentment and joy of spirit. I was quite beside myself, still in spite of that, I knew that I was raised some distance from the Earth, my whole being suspended for a considerable space of time. Down to last Christmas eve (1618) this happened to me on five difference occasions.[1]

One of the greatest influences on my life has been Teresa of Avila. She was a mystic theologian who experienced first-hand all she wrote. She documented the stages of prayer and what the different states of ecstasy felt like. I've read her autobiography[2] over and over again. I take it with me all over the world.

In this story Teresa was preaching and she felt a levitation rapture coming on. She'd already asked her friends to help her if it happened. She was embarrassed!

I felt that the Lord was about to enrapture me again, and once in particular during a sermon - it was at our patron's feast and some great ladies were present - I lay on the ground and the sisters tried to hold me down, but all the same the rapture was observed.[3]

Can you imagine that?! A bunch of nuns jumping on top of her. What must the visiting ladies have thought? It would have looked really funny! Still she was lifted up in the Spirit.

Teresa describes in detail what raptures felt like. It makes me so hungry for God.

The effects of rapture are great. One is that the mighty power of the Lord is manifest. We see that against His Majesty's will we can do nothing to control either the soul or the body. We are not the masters; whether we like it or not, we see there is one mightier than we; that these favours are given by Him, and that, of ourselves we can do absolutely nothing.

She continues:

This imprints a deep humility upon us. I confess that in me it roused a great fear, at first a really great fear. One sees one's body being lifted from the ground; and though the spirit draws it up after itself, and does so most gently if it does not resist, one does not lose consciousness. At least I myself was sufficiently aware to realise I was being lifted up. The majesty of the One who can do this is so manifest that one's hair stands on end, and a great fear comes over one of offending so great a God.

Beautiful!

What I love about Teresa, she wasn't trying to levitate or do anything, other than just falling deeply, madly in love with God. This is the mystic way. It is the way of Love.

St. Francis was a man of incredible integrity who also tried to hide his levitations. Often praying in secluded places, his friends would find him risen high up in the air. Sometimes he flew so high he went out of sight:

(Brother Leo) found St. Francis outside the cell (his room) raised up into the air sometimes as high as three feet, sometimes four, at other times halfway up or at the top of the beech trees - and some of those trees were very high. At other times he found the Saint raised so high in the air and surrounded by such radiance that he could hardly see him.[4]

Catherine of Sienna from a young age frequently levitated. As strange as this sounds to us, she would actually fly up the stairs of her home! Her biographer, Raymond of Capua writes:

Her mother informed me, and Catherine was obliged to acknowledge it to me, that when purposing to mount the staircase she was borne up to the top without touching the steps with her feet, and such was the rapidity of her ascent that the mother trembled lest she fall.[5]

St. Francis of Posadas, a Dominican would often float upwards during Holy Mass:

He once said after returning to the floor that, "I cannot tell whether I left the earth or the earth withdrew from me." Once, after reciting the words of consecration, his body rose in the air and remained suspended. When he finally descended, the congregation saw that he was encompassed by a great light and his face was transformed: his wrinkles had disappeared, his skin was as transparent as crystal and his cheeks were a deep red.[6]

One of the most amusing saints for flights was a man called Joseph from Copertino. He was totally addicted to God and simple things would trigger him into raptures and ecstasies, from seeing a Christmas painting of Jesus, to daily communion. He floated between two and three hours a day. No wonder he's the patron saint of pilots!

During these intense joy-explosions he would shout loudly, then rise, fly around, and even dance in the air. The book of his life by Father Angelo Pastrovicchi, at times reads like a 'Divine Comedy'. It's hilarious!

On one occasion Joseph was present at the investment of several nuns in the church of St. Clare at Copertino. As soon as the choir intoned the antiphon, "Come the bride of Christ," he was seen to hurry from the corner in which he knelt towards the confessor of the convent, a member of the Order of the Reformati, grasp him by the hand, lift him by supernatural power from the floor, and rapidly dance about him in the air.[7]

Sounds like Mary Poppins! I think God enjoys comedy. Think about poor Ezekiel!

Then I saw something that looked like an arm. The arm reached out and grabbed me by the hair on my head. Then the Spirit lifted me into the air (Ez 8:3, ERV).

Crazy stuff. We're going to have a lot of fun things happen in the coming years. Not all of this is deep. Some of it is simply for joy! God is the blissful God (1 Tim 1:11).

Levitation isn't only a Catholic phenomenon. The great healing apostle John G. Lake saw ascension miracles in his meetings. Lake writes:

One evening as I was preaching the Spirit of the Lord descended upon a man in the front row. It was Dr. E. H. Cantel, a minister from London, England. He remained in a sitting posture, but began rising from the chair: gradually he came down on the chair: and again gradually began to rise, somewhat higher, then gradually he came down. This was repeated three times. Was it a reversal of gravitation? I think not. My own conception is that his soul became so united with the Spirit of God that the attractive power of God was so intense it drew him up.[8]

Prophet Bobby Conner also has a funny levitation story. Bobby was ministering abroad in a meeting of thousands. He misjudged the stage end and stepped right off the edge. Amazingly he floated in the air. Alarmed, he quickly stepped back onto the stage. Later on Bobby asked the Lord why this miracle happened. God said he did it to stop Bobby looking stupid!! Hilarious! That's true friendship!

We've also had some fun with levitation. I was in Melbourne Australia, ministering with Ian Clayton. In the morning I could tell by his face that Ian had experienced a special night. Ian had that eternal look again. Ian told us what happened. He said he woke up in the middle of the night and his bed was a few feet up in the air. He was surprised. We laughed about it. It just seemed funny. Ian couldn't explain it!

Whatever we think about this subject, our "KAINOS" race will ultimately ALL know how to levitate. The future is already written in Scripture. We will meet Jesus in the air:

The Master himself will give the command. Archangel thunder! God's trumpet blast! He'll come down from heaven and the dead in Christ will rise - they'll go first. Then the rest of us who are still alive at the time will be caught up with them into the clouds to meet the Master. Oh, *we'll be walking on air*! And then there will be one huge family reunion with the Master. So reassure one another with these words (1 Thes 4:15-18, MSG).

That will be one amazing happy day.

See you in the clouds!

ABOUT THE AUTHOR

Justin Paul Abraham is a popular podcaster and an international speaker known for his joyful teachings on the happy gospel, the mystic realms of God and KAINOS new creation realities. He lives in the UK with his four kids, Josh, Sam, Beth and Oliver, and his inspirational wife, Rachel Abraham.

www.companyofburninghearts.com

SeraphCreative

Heaven's Heart for Earth

Seraph Creative is a collective of artists, writers, theologians & illustrators who desire to see the body of Christ grow into full maturity, walking in their inheritance as Sons Of God on the Earth.

Sign up to our newsletter to know about the release of new books by Justin Paul Abraham as well as other exciting releases.

Visit our website :

www.seraphcreative.org

73635665R00098

Made in the USA
San Bernardino, CA
08 April 2018